INVITATIONS
——TO——
RESPONSIBILITY

INVITATIONS
—TO—
RESPONSIBILITY

*The therapeutic
engagement of
men who are
violent and
a b u s i v e*

Dulwich Centre Publications

Copyright© 1990 by Dulwich Centre Publications
ISBN 0 7316 9621 2

first published 1990
first reprint 1993
second reprint 1997
third reprint 2001

published by, and available from:
Dulwich Centre Publications
Hutt St PO Box 7192
Adelaide 5000
South Australia
phone (61-8) 8223 3966
fax: (61-8) 8232 4441

Printed and Manufactured in Australia
by Graphic Print Group, Richmond, South Australia

"... for whatever a man soweth, that shall he also reap."

Galations 6:7

"I'm not, not, not responsible
not, not, not responsible
I can't answer for the things I do ...
(cos I'm so in love with you)"

sung by Helen Shapiro (1963)

"I think it's more to the right," said Piglet nervously.
"What do you think, Pooh?"
Pooh looked at his two paws. He knew that one of them
was the right, and he knew that when you had decided
which one of them was the right, then the other one was
the left but he could never remember how to begin.
"Well - ", he said slowly.

A.A. Milne, 1928
(The House at Pooh Corner)

ACKNOWLEDGEMENTS

I would like to give special thanks to:

Maxine Joy, for her unique loving, supportive and creative contributions to the writing of this book.

Cheryl White for her remarkable organising skills, enthusiasm and encouragement without which this book would never have been published.

Michael Durrant for editorial assistance and especially for his imaginative and tireless efforts in providing me with irresistable invitations to publish my work.

Rob Hall and Penny Roughan whose comments on drafts of the manuscript were extremely valuable and who, as colleagues, have provided me with inspiration and opportunities to develop this work.

Libby Smith, Judy Shepherd and Ann Chua who typed so many drafts of the initial manuscript and were perhaps as relieved as I was to finally complete the task.

Janine Brett and Alison Turner who magically transformed the text and designed the layout.

Michael Leunig, John Wright and an unknown cartoonist whose sublime drawings say it all.

Many women, men and children who, as clients, cannot be named but who helped me to understand more of the nature of genuine responsibility.

CONTENTS

PART III: THE PROCESS OF ENGAGEMENT OF MEN WHO SEXUALLY ABUSE CHILDREN

PART 1

EXPLANATIONS OF VIOLENT AND ABUSIVE BEHAVIOUR

"The old grey donkey, Eeyore, stood by himself in a thistly corner of the forest, his front feet well apart, his head on one side, and thought about things. Sometimes he thought sadly to himself, "Why?" and sometimes he thought, "Wherefore?" and sometimes he thought, "Inasmuch as which?" - and sometime he didn't quite know what he was thinking about. So when Winnie-the-Pooh came stumping along, Eeyore was very glad to be able to stop thinking for a little, in order to say "How do you do?" in a gloomy manner to him.

"And how are you?" said Winnie-the-Pooh. Eeyore shook his head from side to side. "Not very how," he said. "I don't seem to have felt at all how for a long time."

A.A. Milne (1926) "Winnie-the-Pooh"

INTRODUCTION

Over the past ten years, my colleagues and I have been developing and exploring models for understanding and working with both adolescent and adult male perpetrators of violence and sexual abuse. Our aim has been to develop models of intervention that assist abusive males to cease their abusive behaviour and to relate respectfully to others.

The models are based on the assumption that these goals can best be achieved if the abuse perpetrator accepts full **responsibility** for his abusive actions. In order to accept responsibility, the perpetrator must acknowledge fully the existence and significance of the abuse and understand the potential impact of his abusive actions upon the victim and others. He must accept his culpability for his actions and bear the full onus for ceasing his abuse and changing his behaviour.

In the course of this work, I have become particularly interested in the explanations for abusive behaviour, subscribed to by perpetrators, victims and other persons influenced by the abuse. One of the most frequent questions I am asked by clients and colleagues alike is, "Why did he do it?"

The search for a causal explanation which is inherent in the question "Why?", is an inevitable characteristic of the Western tradition of empirical science. Within this tradition, a problem is best solved by uncovering and rectifying its true underlying cause. Finding the correct and true causal explanation is seen to be helpful in deciding who or what is to blame for the problem, where to attribute responsibility and what action should be taken to solve it. Perpetrators and others influenced by abuse, tend to become extremely preoccupied with the search for a causal explanation of the perpetrator's behaviour. In fact, many people feel distressed, confused and bewildered if they are unable to explain the cause of a problem.

All persons influenced by the abuse adopt particular explanations and ways of thinking about it, as they pursue this inevitable quest, and the explanations adopted will have an important effect on the solutions available to people for dealing with abusive behaviour. I have been struck by the nature of these explanations and the fact that many of them may be unhelpful in that they promote attempts to solve abuse-related problems which are at best misguided and often harmful.

Many explanations of abuse promote an avoidance of responsibility by the perpetrator and an acceptance of responsibility by the victim or others affected by the abuse. Responsibility for the abuse may be attributed to external events and stresses, the actions of others or medical/psychological conditions, over which the perpetrator feels he has little influence or control. This thinking tends to promote unhelpful solutions and often leaves victims of abuse carrying the burdens of shame, guilt and responsibility for their own victimization. Not surprisingly, all members of a family or social system influenced by abuse may feel trapped in a context of abuse in which the perpetrator feels unable to cease his abusive actions, the victim feels unable to seek assistance or leave and other persons feel powerless to intervene.

The search for a causal explanations can be extremely limiting when it serves only to relieve, pacify and excuse the perpetrator of responsibility. Furman and Ahola (1988), quote Maturana's description of an explanation as "a claim that pacifies the wonderer". The perpetrator may "discover" and attribute responsibility to an external cause which was previously concealed from him and so feel a sense of relief, reduced culpability, absolution from guilt, entitlement to forgiveness and permission to make a new start where "all can be forgotten". The discovery of a causal explanation may relieve the abuse perpetrator from the experience of shame and guilt which normally accompanies facing up to, and accepting full responsibility for, his actions.

The quest for a causal explanation itself, can be pacifying for the perpetrator and can become an end in itself. When abuse perpetrators become extensively preoccupied with the search for a cause, they generally do little to take responsibility for and cease their abusive behaviour. They convince themselves and others that they are "trying hard" as they become increasingly bogged down in a kind of introspective "navel-gazing". Further instances of abuse may be responded to by stepping up efforts to locate he true and correct cause - by trying more of the same.

Victims of abuse may become equally preoccupied with the question "Why?" This question may be expressed in the form, "Why me?" or "Why did he do this?" While such questions are inevitable reflections of the victim's experience of grief, they frequently relate to explanations in which the victim believes that s/he shares responsibility for the abuse.

Consequently, the search for causal explanations often leads to ideas which promote blame and the avoidance of responsibility by the perpetrator and prevents the discovery of alternative solutions which are likely to be helpful to both the perpetrator and others influenced by the abuse.

Therapists, too can become preoccupied with causal explanations of abusive behaviour. This inadvertently promotes a similar preoccupation in their clients which excuses the perpetrator of responsibility for the abuse.

Systems theories, based on cybernetic approaches, challenge the empirical tradition and propose new **constructions** of problems which are not based on causal explanation. According to such "constructivist" philosophies, there are no true explanations - only subjective constructions which are created by the observer. Bateson's (1972, 1980) notions of **context** and **restraint** as developed by White (1984, 1986a, 1986b) are particularly useful in explaining abusive behaviour and lead to innovative ideas in therapy. Abuse perpetrators can be seen to hold values and beliefs which act as **restraints** to the acceptance of responsibility for abusive actions and the development of sensitive and respectful relationships with others. These restraints are reflected in the ways that abusive males (and others) construct explanations for their abusive actions and blueprints for relating to others. Restraints are best understood by examining them in the **context** in which they have been developed and are maintained. The behaviour of abuse perpetrators tends to be quite consistent with their restrained views of themselves and their relationships and the context in which they experience and express these views.

It is helpful to explore and understand the explanations and attributions of abusive male clients. The high levels of denial and avoidance of responsibility demonstrated by many abuse perpetrators are understandable in this context. Therapists who feel obliged to challenge this denial or "break it down" without understanding its context may find themselves arguing more strongly for responsibility than their increasingly "resistant" clients. An understanding of the client's explanations and attributions of responsibility is essential for engaging his cooperation and participation in therapy.

EXPLANATIONS OF ABUSE - AND THEIR CONSEQUENCES

In the following chapters, I will examine popular explanations and ways of thinking about abusive behaviour, along with the "solutions" they tend to promote. These explanations and attempted solutions will be examined in the context of the limitations they place on helping the perpetrator to cease his abusive behaviour and to develop respectful and sensitive relationships with others.

A look at the shortcomings of these ways of thinking leads to proposing a model of explanation which I find useful for understanding and intervention with abuse perpetrators and others influenced by the abuse.

TRANSLATING EXPLANATION INTO INTERVENTION

A model of explanation is only useful if the solutions it proposes can be harnessed in an approach to intervention.

I believe that approaches informed by systems theory can offer much to therapists working with abusive men, if they are sensitive to the wider socio-cultural context and can allow therapists to challenge traditional patterns of attributing responsibility for violence. The model of explanation based on a theory of restraint, leads to a model for intervention in therapy which is designed to assist abusive men in ceasing their abusive behaviour and in learning to relate more sensitively, respectfully and equitably with their partners. This work is based on the assumption that these goals can be best achieved if the abuse perpetrator accepts responsibility for his abusive behaviour. This requires the man to acknowledge fully the existence and significance of the abuse and to understand the potential impact of his abusive actions upon his partner and others. It requires him to understand and accept his culpability for his actions and ability to cease his abusive behaviour.

Brennan (1985), Gondolf (1987), Jennings (1987), and Knopp (1984) have reviewed the variety of contemporary approaches to therapy with male spouse abusers and sexual offenders. Most of these approaches acknowledge problems with motivation in abusive men. These include denial that there is a problem with violence or abuse, unwillingness to attend therapy, attending therapy in order to persuade a spouse to reunite or to avoid legal charges once this goal is achieved, and avoidance of responsibility for violence. Not surprisingly, abusive men have often been regarded as "resistant" and unsuitable for therapy.

Seeing these men as resistant is a recipe for therapist frustration and failure. Rather, the challenge is to derive an approach which will engage the man in a way that facilitates his taking responsibility for his participation in therapy and encourages an active interest and motivation in changing his own behaviour. The model for intervention I will propose rests on using the understanding of patterns of attributing responsibility for violence to derive an approach that engages men willingly in therapy. It constitutes a framework for therapy which is based on White's (1986a) "Template for Therapy". I have used this framework in individual, group and couple therapy formats.

John Wright

Alan Jenkins

CAUSAL EXPLANATIONS OF VIOLENCE AND ABUSE

Explanations of abuse, when viewed from a constructivist perspective, are not evaluated in terms of their truth or falseness. They are regarded as subjective attempts to explain abusive behaviour that in turn influence attempts to solve abuse-related problems. Rather than discuss how correct each explanation is, the reader is invited to consider how helpful an explanation is likely to be in assisting the perpetrator of abuse to accept responsibility for the abuse.

Causal explanations of abuse of behaviour may be categorized according to four levels of context:

---------- those that relate to causes which are seen to be located within the individual perpetrator;

---------- those that relate to causes which are seen to be located within the individual's interaction with others;

---------- those that relate to causes which are seen to be located within the individual's developmental history;

---------- those that relate to causes which are seen to be located within Western culture and society.

INDIVIDUAL THEORIES

Explanations which relate to the individual context generally describe the cause of abuse as some form of personality dysfunction or psychopathology within the individual perpetrator. Some of these explanations are discussed below.

Characterological or Personality Theories

Such explanations may refer to qualities of the perpetrator's **character** or personality which are inferred from his behaviour. He may be seen as possessing a character with an **excess** of a principle or quality of abuse.

I've got too much aggro;
He has a violent nature.

A sexually abusive male may be seen as possessing an excess of sexual interest.

He's over sexed;
He'd go after anything in a skirt.

The concept of "deviant sexual arousal" which refers to characteristic genital arousal patterns shown by some sexual offenders, has gained popularity as an explanatory concept amongst behaviourists (Earls 1988; Finkelhor & Araji 1986). It is assumed that the child offender abuses because he experiences deviant arousal towards children. The clinician then targets the deviant arousal as the cause of the problem and attempts to modify it. Such explanations are simple and appealing but can facilitate a blurring of the distinction between the offender's experience of arousal and his abusive actions. Abusive actions are often attributed to excesses of emotional states such as anger or sexual arousal and consequently are seen as natural, inevitable and even unavoidable outcomes of these emotional states. Abusive males, however, must feel able to control their actions, regardless of the intensity of their feelings or emotional states, in order to take responsibility for abuse.

Alternatively, the characterological defect may be seen as a deficit in a particular quality such as "impulse control". Such individuals see themselves or are seen by others as having a low threshold or low tolerance in some critical capacity that relates to the control of violence or sexual behaviour.

I have got a short fuse;
I just went blank - I snapped - I lost control;
I knew it was wrong but I couldn't help myself;
He can't control his sexual urges.

"Impulse control" deficits are commonly referred to in academic explanations of abusive behaviour (Gebhard et al 1965; Marolla & Scully 1979; National Committee on Violence 1990; Summit & Kryso 1978). Such descriptions can be extremely limiting in that they amount to little more than statements that the abuser's behaviour is somewhat uncontrollable. It is difficult to determine just what "impulse control" means, let alone how a man can take responsibility for his abusive behaviour if he has "poor impulse control".

Alan Jenkins

characterological

Characterological explanations sometimes propose a **biological or psychiatric illness** as the basis for the behaviour. There is a good deal of support for theories which describe a biological drives or medical conditions which result in a propensity to violence amongst certain persons:

It runs in the family;
He's sick - crazy - nuts;
He's a psycho.

The notion of an illness or character defect may be appealing as an explanation due to its simplicity. In particular, it may offer relief to the perpetrator by inviting him to attribute blame to a deficient part of himself over which he feels he has little influence. It then becomes the job of an expert to take responsibility and "cure" him. He feels entitled to sympathy and support. Those victimized by his abuse may be invited to accept or tolerate his actions and hence take responsibility for him.

Characterological explanations tend to be somewhat limited in terms of their ability to promote acceptance of responsibility for abusive behaviour by the perpetrator. They generally fail to address the fact that most abusive men are abusive in certain contexts but not in others. There is little evidence to suggest that medical or psychopathological paradigms are appropriate for working with most abusive persons. (Gelles & Cornell 1985; Gondolf 1985). In spite of the shortcomings of characterological explanations, they are extremely popular. Victims of spouse abuse and sexual abuse, when surveyed frequently attribute the cause of the abuse to characteristics of the perpetrator's personality (Queensland Domestic Violence Task Force Report 1988).

Clinical researchers have attempted to delineate **personality profiles** of abuse perpetrators, (see reviews by Langevin 1985; Araji & Finkelhor 1986; Hamberger & Hastings 1986; Hotaling & Sugarman 1986; Gondolf & Hanneken 1987; Levin & Stava 1987; Russell 1988), based on psychological constructs and motives which are inferred from the perpetrator's behaviour and his responses to psychological tests. No unitary profiles can be discerned for spouse abusers, child sexual offenders or other groups of abusers. In attempts to deal with the heterogeneity of the population of abusers, a variety of spouse abuser sub-types, (Gondolf 1985; Russell 1988), rapist sub-types, (Russell 1984) and child sexual offender sub-types (Groth 1982) have been proposed.

These profiles or types are unreliable and have little validity in predicting abusive behaviour. There are, however, common themes which occur frequently in descriptions of offenders, regardless of the nature of their abuse. Many descriptions of abusive males include low self esteem, feelings of inadequacy, fears of insufficiency and inferiority in relationships and with respect to masculine identity. Offenders are seen as having rigid views regarding gender roles and parenting and as maintaining unrealistic and unattainable expectations of their partners, children and themselves. A high level of emotional dependency on others in the family, is often described, along with feelings of insecurity and threat, difficulties with trust, jealousy and a strong desire to control or dominate family members. Abusers are often described as feeling threatened and experiencing others as hostile and rejecting. They may be highly critical of others. Researchers point out that most abusers tend to deny or minimize their abusive behaviour and are prone to projecting blame for problems onto others. Abusers are often described as egocentric individuals who lack empathy for their victims or as showing a "Jekyll and Hyde" personality in which they alternate between anxious concern over the consequences of their abusive actions and disrespect and insensitivity to others.

These characteristics or traits are descriptive of many abuse perpetrators. However, when clustered into "personality profiles" or "personality disorders" and viewed as explanations of abuse, they are static and tautological. (An incest offender, for example, may be seen to abuse because he has a certain fixed personality type or disorder.) As explanations, they often fail to point to solutions at all, let alone promote acceptance of responsibility by the perpetrator.

Theories Relating to Psychological Processes and Motives

Some individual explanations of abuse are framed in a less static manner by referring to individual **psychological processes and motives.**

"Container" theories are popular and typical of such explanations. These theories speculate that abuse perpetrators store up or accumulate emotions such as frustration, tension, anger or sexual arousal, in response to environmental stressors and cues, until a certain threshold is reached, whereupon an "explosion" of abuse results. This process is based on models of pressure and force used in Newtonian physics to describe the functioning of mechanical devices such as steam engines.

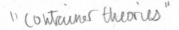
" Container theories "

Alan Jenkins

The perpetrator is likened to a container or tank with a finite capacity which functions in a similar fashion to a mechanical boiler, passively receiving feelings which are "bottled up". These explanations are limited in that they propose a passive process by which the perpetrator is acted upon by factors, such as stress, in his environment. The filling of the container and the abusive behaviour are attributed to external environmental factors (such as work stress, financial pressures and marital problems) over which he has little influence. Consequently, he may not perceive that he has any control of, or responsibility for, the build up or filling of his container, let alone his abusive behaviour. Support for this kind of thinking can be found in popular psychological explanations such as "frustration - aggression" theories which assume a linear relationship between aggressive behaviour and levels of frustration and can encourage the attribution of responsibility for abuse to external stresses (Storr 1970).

Container models suggest solutions which require mechanisms for emptying the container or "letting off steam". Physical activity and relaxation techniques are sometimes indicated for this purpose. Some residential facilities for adolescents provide punching bags for this purpose, to be used when the adolescent gets "worked up" or "hot under the collar". These ideas are popular and are prescribed for violent males, in spite of evidence that links their use to escalations of violent behaviour (Tavris 1982). In all of these "solutions", the process recommenced for emptying the container bears little relationship to the process by which it is seen to fill.

Container theories can promote another kind of misguided and unhelpful confusion. If anger is seen to fill his container, then a violent man may identify the emotion of anger or the experience of conflict as pathological and the problem to be avoided. The solution to violence is then to eliminate anger and conflict. This confusion can restrain the perpetrator from learning to experience anger and conflict in non-violent ways. In my experience, spouse abusers are often quite phobic about anger and conflict, go to great extremes to avoid or escape them and expect their partners to behave in ways which will prevent to conflict.

Some sexual offenders experience escalating urges to abuse which they describe in terms of the container model. The perpetrator may view himself as the passive recipient of an escalating urge which builds up to a point where he feels he is no longer able to contain it. As with spouse abusers, many sexual offenders are unaware of their own contribution to this escalation and either regard their urges as having an independent existence from themselves or see themselves as victims of external influences.

Many such offenders confuse their urges with their abusive actions. They identify the urges as the problem and spend increasing amounts of time trying to avoid, suppress or distract themselves from them, only to find that their urges seem to become more pervasive and intense. In attempting to control or avoid their own feelings and experience, these men find themselves increasingly unsuccessful in making responsible decisions about their actions.

Some abuse perpetrators explain their actions with individual theories of psychological process which are based on the notion of disinhibition. Such theories postulate that conventional inhibitions against abusive behaviour are overcome as a result of intoxication with alcohol or other drugs. The perpetrator may explain:

I was drunk, - I didn't know what I was doing, - I don't remember what happened.

Responsibility is attributed to the disinhibiting substance rather than accepted by the perpetrator himself. Such explanations have gained wide acceptability because drug abuse and person abuse often co-exist (Rada 1976; Walker 1984; Kantor & Straus 1987). However, it is equally plausible to regard both forms of abuse as reflections of the same problem, as it is to regard them as being casually related.

Theories of **blockage** are popular psychological explanations of abusive behaviour (Finkelhor & Araji 1986). These theories propose that normal processes of relating are blocked or unavailable for the perpetrator, generally as a result of certain social skill deficits. Abusive men are frequently described as having poor conflict-management and communication skills (Deschner 1984; Neidig et al 1985). Problem solving and stress management skills are also seen to be deficient (Sonkin et al 1985) It is commonly reported that abusive men lack assertiveness, have difficulty in identifying and expressing feelings and difficulties with intimacy (Groth 1979, 1982; Rosenbaum & O'Leary 1981; Gondolf 1985; Segal & Marshall 1985; Hotaling & Sugarman 1986; Overholser & Beck 1986). By and large, abusive men are seen to experience considerable difficulty in meeting the skill requirements for establishing and maintaining intimate relationships.

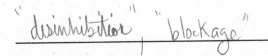

Other blockage theories refer to limitations or deficits as a result of psycho-social or psycho-sexual immaturity or stalled psychological development (Finkelhor & Araji 1986; Gondolf 1987).

Blockage explanations generally promote "solutions" which involve the teaching of social skills to the perpetrator. However useful these attempts may be, they do not necessarily invite the perpetrator to accept responsibility for his abusive behaviour.

There have been some impressive attempts by academics and clinicians to explain abusive behaviour with multi-factorial theories (combinations of individual theories) (e.g., Finkelhor & Araji 1986). Individual theories, however, tend to be limited by their narrow context. They mostly locate the cause of the abusive behaviour within the individual but not often in ways which facilitate the abuser taking responsibility.

INTERACTIONAL EXPLANATIONS OF ABUSE

There is a long history, in the psychological literature, of attempts to explain abusive behaviour within families, by referring to characteristics of the victim, non-abusive family members and patterns of interaction between family members. This tradition is continued in many family therapy approaches in which abuse is regarded as symptomatic of overall family maladjustment and dysfunction. Families in which abuse has been perpetrated have been described as enmeshed, lacking individuation, closed systems, having rigid gender and relationship roles and lacking in generational boundaries (Bograd 1984; Cook & Frantz-Cook 1984; Alexander 1985; Friedman 1988).

Abuse as a Homeostatic or Purposeful Mechanism within Interaction

Interactional explanations are popular amongst clinicians, abuse perpetrators and those influenced by abuse. Some of these explanations regard abusive behaviour as "functional" or as having a **purpose or intent**. Abusive behaviour may be seen as having conscious or unconscious intent either to achieve an instrumental goal or to maintain an unstable family arrangement.

Some spouse abusers regard their violence as a justifiable form of "correction" of their partner. Aspects of their partner's behaviour are regarded as inexcusable, disloyal, disrespectful or stupid and hence requiring correction. When all else has failed to correct her "errant" behaviour, violence may be regarded as the last resort. These men who act from a stance of greater perceived authority, are likely to entertain thoughts such as the following, whilst engaging in violence:

I'll shake some sense in to her;
I'll teach her a lesson she won't forget.

Some violence may be seen to be justified by a need for vindication or vengeance - to get back or even the score:

I'll bring her down from her high horse;
I'll cut her down to size;
She doesn't look so smart now.

These thoughts are based on rigid notions of right and wrong and idiosyncratic beliefs about truth, justice and fairness which must be pursued at any cost. Some spouse abusers regard their violence, as necessary for the establishment of respect and intimacy in their relationships. One such perpetrator explained:

Its the only time we talk and have good sex.

The existence of conscious or unconscious intent in physical abuse is postulated in many academic theories. Physical violence has been described as having an homeostatic function in helping to maintain an inequality of power and status in complimentary, "dominant - submissive" relationships (Weitzman & Dreen 1982). Violence has also been described as having an homeostatic function in regulating the balance of closeness and distance in relationships where individual boundaries are blurred (Cook & Frantz-Cook 1984). Relationship types such as the "underadequate husband - overadequate wife" have been proposed in which the wife is seen to be verbally more competent and critical of her partner who in turn feels powerless and resorts to violence to rectify the perceived imbalance of power (Hoffman 1981).

Abuse victims have even been described as wanting to be abused as a result of various unconscious motivations. Spouse abuse victims have been described as bringing on their own abuse and even as "masochistic" (Snell et al 1964). Some spouse abusers are puzzled by their partner's impotent and despairing behaviour:

She just stood there and told me to hit her.

In a similar way, the naive or coerced participation of victims of child sexual abuse has been described as "seductive" and "pseudo-mature" and as compensating for the mother's dysfunctional behaviour (Lustig et

Alan Jenkins

al 1966; Raphling et al 1967; Justice & Justice 1979). Sexual offenders may explain:

She wanted me to do it - she used to initiate it;
If she had said "No", I would have stopped.

The abusive actions of some spouse abusers and rapists have been conceptualized as purposeful and motivated by "sadism", contempt for women and a desire to seek punishment and revenge (Yourell & McCabe 1988). Abusers are often described as lacking in a sense of power and control in their own lives and relationships (Finkelhor 1983; Gondolf 1985). Abusive actions may be seen to be motivated by an intent to compensate for feelings of inadequacy and powerlessness (Gondolf & Hanneken 1987) or to establish dominance and authority and gain control by humiliating the victim and attempting to reduce her status (Dobash & Dobash 1979).

Theories of purpose or intent are not uncommon in interactional explanations of incestuous abuse of children. In many of these theories the mother is described as a weak, ineffective and inadequate woman who is unable to meet the requirements of her role as a wife or mother and who "colludes" with the abuse by allowing her daughter to take on certain aspects of her role. Having exchanged roles, with her daughter, the mother participates in maintaining a family secret. In this way, incest is regarded as "functional" in holding an unstable family together (Lustig et al 1966; Machotka et al 1967; Rist 1979; Will 1983). The mother-daughter relationship is seen as critical in many explanations of incestuous abuse. The incest victim may be seen as accepting the incest as a substitute for her dysfunctional mother's inadequate nurturance, love and protection.

Larson & Maddock (1986) have described a "typology of incest families based on the "function that the incest serves in a given family system".

An abusive adolescent's behaviour may be regarded as "functional" in distracting his parents' attention from their marital problems and uniting their concern in the service of helping their son. In this way an unstable marriage can be maintained (Haley 1963).

Abuse as a Consequence of Dysfunctional Interaction

Another group of interactional theories suggest that abusive behaviour is not purposeful or "functional" but simply an inevitable consequence of dysfunctional patterns of relating within a family.

Most of these explanations propose that abuse occurs as a result of provocation by the victim or by some other person. Consequently, spouse abuse may be explained and justified as behaviour provoked by the perpetrator's wife:

She asked for it;
She had it coming;
What else could I do - she wouldn't listen;
She pushed me too far.

The abuse victim may even share this belief in provocation and remark:

I deserved it;
I guess I had it coming to me;
How can I stop upsetting my husband?

The violent adolescent may self-righteously explain:

He called me a dickhead;
She turned off the TV during my favorite show.

A sexual offender may see himself as having been provoked by the "seductive" behaviour exhibited by the victim or the withholding of sex by his wife. Rape victims are sometimes seen as "asking for it". An adolescent rapist explained:

If she didn't want to go all the way, she shouldn't have started it in the first place.

Victims of sexual assault may even regard themselves as provoking abuse:

What did I do to encourage him/lead him on;
I shouldn't have talked to him/gone out with him.

Interactional explanations are commonly used, by clinicians and parents, to explain abusive behaviour in adolescents or children, (Madden 1982). Many parents fear that they are in some way the cause of their offspring's abusive behaviour. Parents may be seen as too strict or even abusive and neglectful or alternatively not strict enough and not having set enough limits. Alternatively, they may be viewed as inconsistent in setting limits. Adolescents are quick to attribute responsibility, for their own abusive behaviour, to their parents who are in turn likely to feel considerable guilt.

Alan Jenkins

Explanations of consequence often lead to unhelpful patterns of thinking such as the confusion between violence and conflict. Physical abuse often occurs in a context of escalating conflict between spouses (Straus et al 1980). Consequently, many spouse-abuse perpetrators and their partners regard violence as an inevitable consequence of an escalating argument in which neither partner will back down. This theory suggests that physical violence is a natural and unavoidable progression from the verbal expression of conflict and that conflict will turn into violence once a certain threshold is reached. Violence is seen as a quantitative step rather than a qualitative leap, in an argument. This belief is extremely restraining for the couple who can not feel free to argue without there being a risk of violence.

It is clear that interactional explanations can describe relationship patterns and dynamics which are of considerable interest to clinicians. As explanations of the cause of abusive behaviour, however, they are considerably limited. By locating the cause of the abuse within dysfunctional patterns of relating, responsibility or blame may be shared with or even totally attributed to the victim or other family members. Interactional explanations do not invite the perpetrator to accept full responsibility for his abusive behaviour. Feminist theorists have strongly criticized family therapy approaches based on interactional explanations because they fail to address abuse within a socio-cultural context and because they fail to regard the perpetrator as totally responsible for his abusive behaviour (Bograd 1984; McIntyre 1984).

DEVELOPMENTAL THEORIES OF ABUSE

Many academic theories of abuse locate explanations within the developmental history of the perpetrator (and the victim and other family members). Some abuse perpetrators explain their actions by referring to past experiences.

My dad always beat me when I was a kid.

I was sexually abused myself when I was a child.

Social learning theories describe violence in terms of learned behaviour rather than psychopathology or character defect. Abusive behaviour is seen to be passed along families from generation to generation. Each generation learns about abuse by participating in an abusive family. Psychological mechanisms such as modelling and reinforcement of violent behaviour are seen to mediate this learning.

These theories draw on research which indicates that significant percentages of spouse and child abusers have either experienced or witnessed abusive behaviour within their families. (Gelles 1980; Rosenbaum & O'Leary 1981; Perry et al 1983; Telch & Lindquist 1984; Rosenbaum 1986). Sexual offenders report unusually high percentages of childhood sexual victimization (Groth & Burgess 1979; de Young 1982).

Elaborate individual theories of psychological process are sometimes combined with developmental explanations of abuse. Child sexual abuse perpetrators who were sexually abused themselves as children, may engage in a process of "identification with the aggressor". The abuser is seen to compensate for feelings of powerlessness and inadequacy associated with his victimization, by bullying or abusing others who are vulnerable and powerless, in a desperate effort to establish a sense of control and adequacy in his own life. (Groth et al, 1982).

Researchers, in their attempts to delineate characteristics of the families of male abuse perpetrators, have come up with a variety of diverse descriptions ranging from chaotic, disorganized, neglectful and unsupportive to enmeshed and overprotective. (Madden 1982).

Learning theorists have described some of the behaviour of abusive males in terms of direct training and practice in abuse. Abusive behaviour may be reinforced or rewarded by getting one's own way or with sexual gratification. Some sexual offenders practice regularly by masturbating to fantasies of exploitative sexual behaviour (McGuire et al 1965; Saunders & Awad 1988).

Whilst developmental theories may be of intrinsic interest, they do not necessarily invite the abuse perpetrator to take responsibility for his abusive actions. In fact, they can distract the perpetrator from this task, by inviting him to immerse himself in examination of his past experience. Some perpetrators regard developmental explanations as excuses or justifications for their behaviour and see themselves as victims of their pasts with limited options for change in the present. Explanations become facile and unhelpful when they consist of statements like the following: *I was abused as a child and this is why I abused my son.*

SOCIO-CULTURAL THEORIES

Socio-cultural explanations locate the causes of abuse within the social structures, traditions, norms and ideologies of the culture.

Alan Jenkins

Some of these theories posit that violence is built into the structure of Western society and the nuclear family (Gelles et al 1980; Gelles & Cornell 1985). The organization of families in modern society is described as conflict-ridden and social stresses such as unemployment, poverty, homelessness, isolation and over-crowding are seen to predispose individuals to abusive behaviour. Violence and abusive behaviour are seen to be supported, sanctioned and institutionalized in the family and society.

Feminist theory has focused extensively on gender based inequalities of power, privilege and status within society and the family, as a cause of male abuse. Notions of male dominance and ownership and female subservience are seen to be reinforced by patriarchal social structures and an ideology of inferiority of women (Dobash & Dobash 1979; Klein 1981; Schechter 1982; Bograd 1984).

These theories propose that men are systematically socialized into violence as a problem solving technique and as a means of maintaining privilege in a sexist society. Consequently, they learn to resort to the power of their fists or their genitals to achieve these goals. Whilst the individual motivations of abusers may be varied, violence and sexual assault serve as ways of demonstrating, power, control and ownership over family members and therefore maintain the patriarchal social structure.

Socio-cultural theories of abuse point to the need for change in social structures, cultural norms and ideologies in order to stop abusive behaviour. Some theorists consider the issue of the individual's responsibility for his violence as an irrelevant consideration, given the pervasive influence of socio-cultural factors.

According to this model, explanations or theories of abusive behaviour can be evaluated using three pragmatic criteria:

---------- Does the explanation help the perpetrator of the abuse to take full responsibility for his abusive actions?

---------- Does the explanation "point to" plausible and accessible solutions for ceasing the abuse and resolving abuse-related problems.

---------- Is the explanation sensitive to all levels of context, from the individual to the socio-cultural in which the abuse occurs?

Explanations which are useful, invite the perpetrator to take responsibility, point to solutions and relate to all levels of context. They locate the abuse in a variety of contexts and have social relevance as well as clinical usefulness.

The causal explanations and theories previously reviewed have differing degrees of usefulness when judged according to these criteria. Some, in fact, can be quite unhelpful. Causal explanations tend to be based on questions like the following:

---------- What causes Jack to abuse his wife?

---------- Why do men abuse women and children?

Such questions lead to **theories of limitation** in which abuse is seen to be caused by limitations which exist in individuals, families or society. Such theories invite individuals to consider themselves as passive victims of circumstance, driven by internal or external forces towards abusive behaviour. Consequently they become increasingly preoccupied with their own limitations and helplessness. Causal explanations tend to compete with one another for truth and foster the attribution of blame to the limitations which are seen to cause the problem. Such explanations can have a self-fulfilling nature. When violence or abuse is regarded as an acknowledged or accepted response to stress, marital conflict etc. then these factors become "causes" of abuse.

Alan Jenkins

I have found it helpful to use a model which is based on a theory of restraint or negative explanation (Bateson 1972, 1980; White 1984, 1986a, 1986b) which generates questions like the following:

---------- What is stopping Jack from taking responsibility to relate respectfully, sensitively and equitably with his wife?

---------- What is stopping Jack from taking responsibility for his abusive behaviour?

This theory is based on the assumption that males will relate respectfully, sensitively and non abusively with others, unless restrained from doing so. Restraints are traditions, habits, and beliefs which influence the ways that abusive males make sense of and participate in the world. They include factors which can prevent these men from taking responsibilities to establish respectful and sensitive relationships in some contexts and from accepting responsibility for their abusive behaviour. Abusive males generally behave in ways which are quite consistent with their restrained views of the world.

According to this model, restraints do not cause abusive behaviour. When active and influential in mens' lives, they can prevent these men from accepting responsibility for their own actions. Whilst it is true that highly restrained men are more likely to engage in abusive behaviour, the presence of restraining ideas does not guarantee that the man will abuse. For example, a man who was abused himself as a child, who is experiencing considerable financial and marital stress and who at times drinks heavily, may not behave abusively and may relate respectfully to others in his family. If he does abuse, however, there is potential for the development of restraining ideas which foster the attribution of responsibility for his actions to external factors.

A theory of restraint tends to promote an active consideration of alternatives to abuse and what has been stopping the male from engaging in them. He is invited to become pre-occupied with his own competence in challenging restraining habits and ideas and discovering and practicing alternatives to abuse. He is always considered to be responsible for his abusive behaviour and his contribution to relationships and is discouraged from attributing blame and responsibility externally.

Restraints may be examined at the four different levels of context. It may be noted in the following discussion of differing restraints, that some suggestions about ideas that operate as restraints appear little different from some of the factors used as the basis of the explanations in the previous chapter (which, it was suggested, were unhelpful). The important distinction is that between explanation and restraint. There is a difference between proposing factors as causes or explanations, with the implication that they somehow "excuse" behaviour, and proposing similar ideas as factors that restrain men from taking responsibility for their behaviour.

SOCIO-CULTURAL RESTRAINTS

Western industrialized society is characterized by its highly competitive and hierarchical nature and an ideology of individualism or individual achievement, as opposed to co-operation and inter-dependence (Levine 1986; Taubman 1986; Sommers-Flanagan & Walters 1987).

Individual self-esteem and personal success tend to be based on a lust for status and power and the deification of these concepts. Such a recipe for individual status and success promotes the acquisition of property and of control and influence over others and the environment. This ideology is well stated in a commonly used metaphor which refers to feeling good about one's self as, 'being on top of the world'.

This "status-lust" ideology fits with the notion of structuring society into a hierarchical series of "superior - subordinate" relationships. (Sommers-Flanagan & Waters 1987). "Superiors" have acquired greater status and are entitled to greater privilege as well as respect and deference from those in "subordinate" roles. These values are enshrined in the hierarchical relationships of our political, economic, familial and educational systems.

The lust for status and entitlement is often pursued with little regard or responsibility for the impact of these strivings on the welfare of others and the environment. In the pursuit of status or individual success, it is acceptable and even admirable to be 'aggressive' and to exploit or take advantage of others 'weaknesses', in order to gain the upper hand or the 'competitive edge'. This philosophy is evident in the worlds of political, business and personal dealings. Those in "superior" roles understand that they may need to defend their position against competitors. The world becomes conceptualized as a place where individuals are either winners or losers, competing in an arena in which 'might is right'.

This blueprint for individual success tends to promote notions of ownership of "subordinates" by "superiors" and the right to exercise

Alan Jenkins

33

power over "subordinates" for the fulfillment of individual needs. It promotes competitive values at the expense of co-operative relationship values such as empathy, respect, nurturance, trust, sensitivity, sharing, altruism and equity. (Sommers-Flanagan & Waters 1987).

Structures, norms and ideology which promote the individual pursuit of status and entitlement at the expense of responsibility for the welfare of others, are highly restraining influences for the development of respectful and sensitive relationships.

Certain forms of violence and sexual exploitation are legitimized and sanctioned in our culture if they are seen to further a "noble" cause or provide a means to a "higher" end. Violence has often been used to defend or establish a political ideology or state. At such times individuals may be seen somewhat paradoxically as 'fighting for peace'. Violence has frequently been sanctioned in order to punish criminal offenders or political dissenters. Violence and sexual exploitation are legitimized and sanctioned as entertainment in sport, books and movies and in advertising (Roy 1982).

Our educational, legal, political and religious systems often fail to promote the attribution of responsibility for abusive behaviour to the perpetrator of that abuse, by failing to provide the necessary responses and sanctions. There is a historical absence of clear cut legal prohibitions and penalties for the perpetrators of abusive behaviour (Russell 1984; Prepper 1984). This is well evidenced in the following recent examples:

--------- Two fourteen year old boys who forcibly raped a girl at school were suspended for a fortnight for "sexual harassment", whilst the girl felt obliged to leave the school. The educational authorities were initially more concerned about protecting the boys "right to an education" than the rights and safety for girls at the school.

---------- A fifteen year old girl who was sexually abused by an older family member was required to sit in a segregated area in her church because the authorities feared she may 'pollute' other males in the congregation.

---------- Our legal system deals with child sexual abuse allegations using an adversarial process in which a child's witness (and intellect) is pitted against that of the alleged adult offender.

---------- In our legal system, it "pays" for a child sexual abuse offender to deny his offences and call the child a liar because he is more likely to be punished if he takes some responsibility by acknowledging his guilt.

---------- A rape victim was advised by the Police to move to another state and change her name to avoid recrimination by the convicted rapist.

---------- Spouse abuse and child sexual assault victims are often obliged to leave their homes for their own safety, following notification of the abuse. The abuse perpetrator is not required to leave the home.

---------- A newspaper report of a court judgement regarding a domestic homicide was titled, 'Wife Nags Herself to Death'.

Western society and culture tolerates social inequities, values profit at others' expense and legitimizes or fails to respond to certain forms of abuse, and consequently promotes values which are highly restraining to the development of mutuality, sensitivity and respect in relationships and the attribution of responsibility for abusive behaviour to the perpetrator of the abuse.

Socio-cultural Restraints within the Family

The family is a system which requires special focus when considering restraint and responsibility for abusive behaviour. The family is the social system where the failure to attribute responsibility to abuse perpetrators is probably most apparent. Within the family, the traditional distribution of status has been along gender and age lines. Husbands have traditionally been regarded as "superior" to wives, males to females and parents to children. Those in "superior" roles have traditionally been attributed ownership rights over those in "subordinate" roles and have been seen as entitled to greater privilege and deference and respect from "subordinates". "Subordinates" have been expected to maintain the status quo by demonstrating loyalty and support to "superiors". In fact, a traditional criterion for individual success in the family has been the maintenance of loyalty, deference and respect from "subordinates". This promotes a reliance of "superiors" upon "subordinates" to maintain support and thus take responsibility for the maintenance of the "superiors"' self esteem.

There are long-standing historical and legal precedents which have sanctioned and legitimized violence and sexual exploitation of "subordinates" by "superiors", within families (Rush 1980; Schechter 1982;

Prepper 1984; Gelles & Cornell 1985). Traditionally, "superiors" have had the right to chastise or discipline "subordinates" using physical violence, if they do not fulfil their 'obligations'. These rights have been challenged only in recent times with regard to marital violence and marital rape and are still widely accepted in the discipline of children. Such discipline has traditionally been regarded as a necessary and appropriate means to an end. "Superiors" have felt entitled to obedience. In fact, physical violence has been equated with love and caring:

This will hurt me more than it hurts you;
I am doing this because I love you.

Not surprisingly, the victims of such discipline are regarded and may even regard themselves as responsible for "bringing it on themselves".

Recent surveys indicate that significant percentages of both males and females regard physical violence in marriage as acceptable in certain circumstances. (Gentemann 1984; Greenblatt 1985; Public Policy Research Centre 1988; Margolin et al 1989). Large numbers of males and females in non-clinical surveys indicate experience of violence and coerced sexual activity in dating relationships (Stets & Pirog-Good 1989). High percentages (40% - 50% of males in some studies) indicate approval of coerced sexual activity in dating relationships and attribute responsibility to victims of rape in a variety of circumstances (Margolin et al 1989). Margolin's research led her to conclude that, "as couples progress from a first date to marriage, men gain support to violate their partner's consent".

Research on community attitudes to child abuse reveals that child victims are also regarded as partly responsible for their own victimization under certain circumstances (Roscoe et al 1985; Broussard & Wagner 1988).

These attitudes when combined with the ideology of the privacy, harmony and sanctity of the family and family life, reduce the likelihood of external intervention to stop abuse and reality testing by victims of abuse and other family members. (Straus et al 1980; Gelles & Cornell 1985). 'Accommodation syndromes' in abuse victims have been well documented and reflect the successful attribution of responsibility for abuse to the victim rather than the perpetrator (Finkelhor 1983). The important role of secrecy in the maintenance of these patterns of attribution, cannot be over-emphasized.

When does violence or sexual behaviour, within a family context, constitute abuse and exploitation? Any member of a family can be violent or can behave sexually towards another member. Men, women and children in normal families are reported to engage in acts of violence (Gelles et al 1980). Some violent and sexual behaviours are seen as normal and predictable aspects of the development of children. Violence is evident in tantrums, sibling rivalry and the establishment of pecking orders amongst children. Sexual curiosity and experimenting are regarded as normal between children in certain circumstances (Leitenberg et al 1989).

Violence and sexual behaviour have the potential to become persistent, intimidating and exploitative and hence abusive when perpetrated by individuals occupying "superior" roles in which they have greater attributed status or power, greater physical strength and greater access to resources and knowledge. Abuse of any kind is characterized by a more powerful person taking advantage of a less powerful person (Finkelhor 1983). The abuser's sense of entitlement overrides his or her sense of responsibility for the welfare and needs of the victim. The victim of the abuse generally experiences some form of entrapment and feels unable to leave the context of the abuse. The perpetrator generally feels diminished responsibility for the abuse while the victim may assume some of this responsibility. Not surprisingly, the distribution of abuse corresponds to the distribution of status, both in families and in the wider community (Finkelhor 1983; Prepper 1984).

Alan Jenkins

Given the high prevalence of physically and sexually abusive behaviour perpetrated by males, it is useful to examine socio-cultural restraints which relate to **gender.** Traditional patterns of gender role socialization for men (and women) promote values that are highly restraining for the development of respect and sensitivity in relationships and the acceptance of responsibility for abusive behaviour, by males.

Traditions, habits and beliefs which promote an imbalance between males and females in perceived status and entitlement and in responsibility for the social and emotional climate of relationships (social-emotional responsibility), are seen as highly restraining for the development of respectful, sensitive and equitable relationships. (Social-emotional responsibilities include responsibilities for intimacy, nurturance, conflict resolution, empathy and sensitivity to others' needs and feelings, awareness and respect of others' rights and emotional awareness and expression).

These traditions, habits and beliefs are well documented and remain influential in contemporary marital relationships (Krausz 1986; Baxter 1988). They prescribe restraints for males which include:

---------- an exaggerated sense of entitlement and status in relation to females and children.

---------- An avoidance of social-emotional responsibilities.

---------- A reliance on others (especially females) to face social-emotional responsibilities.

Traditional recipes for male self-esteem and success include the acquisition of status and power both within and outside the family. Traditionally, males have been regarded as superior to females and have occupied positions of dominance within the family with entitlement to exert a kind of ownership over family members who could be regarded as "property". In this role, the male could expect obedience, submission and deference from others who take a back seat in decision making. He is not required to countenance any challenge to his authority and is entitled to expect support from other family members. Any challenge to his authority may be seen as deviant or disloyal.

Allegiance to an ideology of ownership and superiority promotes social-emotional avoidance and reliance on others to face these responsibilities. The man's recipe for negotiation or conflict resolution is based on his reliance on others within the family to prevent conflict.

Traditional recipes for masculinity which are consistent with the gender division of responsibility and labor, also foster social-emotional avoidance and reliance. According to traditional gender roles, the male has the responsibility of the economic provider. He must perform, achieve and compete in the outside world of work. His partner's traditional area of responsibility lies within the family - to nurture and take care of domestic duties. Consequently, a man may expect his partner to do the work within the family and feel entitled to be "left in peace" and not "hassled" or "nagged" by her.

This traditional role prescribes an avoidance of intimacy, nurturance and relationship responsibilities by the male. He is not required to be emotionally expressive but expected to be calm and cool in any crisis so that he can take the lead, solve problems in a rational way and not let feelings get in the way. He may be a man of actions rather than words. He is expected to be tough and competitive. He must also be guarded and defensive and not make himself vulnerable by taking emotional risks in which he "lays himself open" or "gives himself away". This gender stereotype is in fact a recipe for social and emotional incompetence and total reliance on a female partner for the social and emotional requirements of relationships.

The relationship and intimacy skills promoted by the traditional female role stereotype, relate to parenting, nurturing, empathy, sensitivity and emotional expressiveness. A woman may develop verbal skills and must take on the responsibility of removing or resolving emotional problems within the family. In fact, it is her obligation to nurture others and alleviate their emotional burdens. Her happiness comes from fulfilling others' needs and she alone, is responsible for the success or failure of marriage or family relationships.

Since she is responsible for the family emotional climate, she is obliged to work hard to keep the family calm and to prevent stress, disharmony and conflict. If there is disharmony then it is her responsibility. Consequently, other family members may rely on her to monitor their behaviour, remove stresses, "walk on egg shells" around them and otherwise protect them from pressures of day to day living.

Gender role prescriptions can be seen to be highly restraining influences for abusive males taking responsibility for their abusive behaviour (Schechter 1982). Abusive males tend to take little responsibility for monitoring and regulating their own abusive behaviour and often

Alan Jenkins

attribute responsibility to their partners for incidents of abuse. Partners of abusive males may believe that they are responsible for preventing and controlling the man's abusive behaviour and for the consequences of the abuse. This is evident when some victims of incestuous abuse appear to be less forgiving of and attribute more blame to their mothers for not protecting them, than to their fathers for abusing them.

Traditional gender stereotypes also provide highly restraining influences on male sexual behaviour (Gross 1978; Zilbergeld 1978; Person 1980; Hite 1981; Metcalf & Humphries 1985). These restraints have special relevance for the consideration of abusive sexual behaviour of males (Russell 1984; Finkelhor & Lewis 1988).

Traditional recipes for male self-esteem and success include notions of sexual conquest and performance. Such notions promote highly restraining habits and beliefs, which include a sense of male sexual entitlement, avoidance of social-emotional responsibilities with respect to sexuality and intimacy and a reliance on partners to take these responsibilities.

These restraints are reflected in beliefs and traditions regarding male sexual entitlement and ownership of the partner's body. The female partner should be available and is expected to provide for the male's sexual needs. Many men are in fact convinced that they must have sex at a certain frequency, otherwise some dreadful consequence will befall them. This emphasis on entitlement promotes a reliance on the partner who is held responsible for meeting the man's sexual needs.

Sexual conquest and performance are traditional criteria for male self-esteem and reflect more general notions of male competition and performance in the wider sphere. Russell (1984), refers to this aspect of male gender role as the "virility mystique". According to the traditional blueprint, men are meant to be virile and to experience sexual desire when attracted by a woman (the "object" of desire) who has cultivated a captivating sexual display. A large, ever-ready, ever-lasting, weapon-like and infallible penis is a necessary accoutrement, in order to act on this desire. The male with his superior knowledge is then able to orchestrate sex and "turn on" his partner. The partner's sexuality will be experienced more as a response to the male's initiative, rather than as desire in its own right.

According to traditional gender recipes, the partner will be younger, smaller, innocent, naive, deferring, inexperienced, virginal and will not challenge the man's authority. Finkelhor & Lewis (1988), refer to the consequences of this preference as the "sexualization of subordination". It is noteworthy that this traditional recipe for a female sexual partner seems more a recipe for a child than one for an adult female.

According to this recipe, conquest or the gaining of access to women and the performance of astonishing sexual feats are all-important in sex. Many men think in quantitative metaphors. Sexual activity is referred to as "scoring". Sexual pre-occupations relate to questions of how often? How many? How long? How big? Quantity appears to more relevant than quality. The partner must be "satisfied" according to the man's definition and criteria for satisfaction. Sex and love may be associated with aggression in this context. There are a variety of scenarios presented in popular literature and popular culture in which sexual activity is seen as an aggressive act performed with a penis which is described as a weapon or assaultive object (Zilbergeld 1978).

This recipe for sexual success promotes a high level of sexual preoccupation and a tendency for men to separate their sexual experience

Alan Jenkins

from an interpersonal or emotional context. The man is expected to be able to perform under any circumstances and sex may appear to take on an independent life of its own. Penises are sometimes as seen as having minds of their own which are somewhat separate from their owner's. In this context, it is not surprising that pornography for males is far more prevalent than pornography for females, given that the recipe promotes a tendency to objectify the partner ("the sex object") and to lack empathy for her feelings. An excessive focus on sexual conquest and performance tends to promote high levels of self-centered sexual pre-occupation and a tendency to avoid social-emotional responsibility in relationships.

In a context where emotional expression is restrained, one of the few permissible emotional options for establishing intimacy is the expression of sexual arousal and sexual feelings. Consequently, the expression of sexual interest becomes a major way of attempting to establish and contribute to intimacy in relationships. This leads to a tendency to "sexualize" needs for affirmation and closeness. The tendency to "over-sexualize" emotional needs is evident as a restraint to accepting responsibility for abusive behaviour with many sexual offenders. Some sexual offenders deal with experiences such as loneliness by contacting prostitutes or seeking other forms of impersonal sex. Many sexual offenders engage in a higher frequency of impersonal sexual behaviour and sexual experience than non-offenders (Kanin 1985).

This notion is reflected in the explanations of some child sexual offenders:

I loved her too much.

I was only trying to love her.

In a similar way, some sexual harassment offenders explain their actions as attempts to establish relationships or intimacy with their victims. Rapists have even been known to make proposals of marriage to their victims after the offence (Russell 1974).

The recipe for sexual conquest and performance acts as a restraint to men's view of their role in relationships and results in a tendency for men to avoid social-emotional responsibility for their own sexual behaviour and rely on women to take this responsibility. Traditionally, it has been the woman's responsibility to set limits in potential or actual sexual encounters and to act as "moral guardians". The traditional male task is to test these limits and find ways around them in order to make a conquest. If the woman seems to be unwilling, then she needs persuasion or even coercion. The scenario of the unwilling woman who really wants the sexual encounter in spite of herself, is coerced into it and then has a remarkable sexual experience for which she is eternally grateful, is well represented in modern fiction and movies (Zilbergeld 1978).

Traditionally, women are seen as responsible for the sexual interest that they "attract". The woman attracts the male's attention and arouses him and once he is aroused, he has no choice but to follow through with sexual activity. The woman is thus considered responsible for the consequences of her initial attractiveness. The dilemma for the woman, in the context of these traditional gender roles, is that she must attract male attention but at the same time avoid "leading males on", appearing "easy" or being a "prick teaser". It is not surprising that many victims of sexual assault accept some responsibility for the behaviour of their assaulter and ask:

What did I do/wear to provoke it?

Traditional gender recipes prescribe that social and emotional responsibilities in relationships should be accepted by female partners. Female sexual partners may not only feel obligation to be available but also to respond to please their partners, regardless of their own feelings. In other words, there may be an obligation to protect the male partner's feelings whilst sacrificing their own needs.

Patterns of abusive behaviour are generally quite consistent with the dictates of traditional gender roles (Schechter 1982; Russell 1984; Parker & Parker 1986; Finkelhor & Lewis 1988). In fact, Russell (1984), regards male rapists, child sexual offenders and sexual harassers as over-conforming, as opposed to deviant, in the context of traditional male gender roles. She cites evidence to support the notion of a continuum of coercive sexual behaviour from that which is considered normal and condoned, to that which is regarded as unacceptable or illegal. This evidence is based on surveys of attitudes of normal men and women to the use of coercion in sex (See also Check & Malamuth 1983; Jenkins & Dambrot 1987). Similar evidence has already been cited with respect to attitudes regarding physical violence towards children and marriage partners.

The theory of restraint is helpful in understanding the inconsistent and contradictory research evidence on the relationship between sex-role stereotyping and abusive behaviour in males. There is a large body of evidence which supports the view that abusive males have attitudes which are highly sex-role stereotyped (Burt 1980; Koss et al 1985; Malamuth 1986; Overholser & Beck 1986; Lisak & Roth 1988; Yourell & McCabe 1988). There is another body of evidence which contradicts these findings (Sattem et al 1984; Rosenbaum 1986; Gondolf & Henneken 1987).

It is helpful to consider gender role stereotyping as a restraining influence on abusive men as apposed to a static condition which influences all abusive men in the same manner and which causes abusive behaviour. Gender role stereotypes prescribe a variety of ideas and behaviours which are in fact quite inconsistent and contradictory and which promote "gender role strain" (Taubman 1986). Recent evidence suggests that many abusive men have "undifferentiated" gender roles whereby they lack a clear gender identity. They regard themselves as failing in masculine pursuits and achievement. Consequently, they are seen to adopt behaviour patterns that are consistent with conceptions of what a man should be like (Groth & Cohen 1976; Rosenbaum 1986; Taubman 1986; Gondolf & Hanneken 1987).

Many abusive men do not regard themselves as having sexist or gender-stereotyped attitudes regarding women or children. They see themselves as egalitarian and fair in their dealings with family members and often feel quite powerless even regarding their partners as oppressive, controlling and unfair.

A theory of restraint helps to explain the varied and pervasive influences of gender-role stereotypes and the heterogeneity in the population of abusive men. Male abusers may range from quiet, passive men who tend to withdraw from conflict to domineering patriarchs who engage in frequent displays of power and status. Gender-prescribed patterns of exaggerated entitlement and social-emotional avoidance and reliance are evident, however, in both of these extremes.

Traditional gender roles are particularly restraining for abusive males in taking responsibility for their abusive behaviour. In all forms of abuse, the abuser tends to focus on his own intent and his own feelings and so lacks empathy or understanding of the effects of his actions upon the victim. The victim is treated as an object, dehumanized and his or her normal rights are disallowed. This lack of empathy is accompanied by justifications and an external attribution of responsibility. The abuser relies on the victim to put up with the consequences of this exploitation and take responsibility for his feelings and needs. The victim is generally expected to keep the abuse secret and, in a variety of ways, take responsibility for the male's behaviour (Finkelhor 1983; Sommers-Flanagan & Walters 1987).

Traditional gender based differentials in status and entitlement and in roles and responsibilities for the maintenance of relationships and family life are highly restraining for both men and women developing respectful and sensitive relationships. They promote an avoidance of social and emotional responsibility in men and a reliance on women to take responsibility for aspects of family life including intimacy, parenting and conflict resolution.

Traditional gender differentials promote a sense of entitlement at the expense of social and emotional responsibility in men. In the context of abusive behaviour, these gender based differentials fail to promote the acceptance of responsibility for abusive behaviour by the perpetrator of that abuse. Instead they encourage the attribution of responsibility to the victim and/or the offender's partner.

There are various movements in our culture which are challenging the ideology of individual entitlement and the differentials inherent in traditional gender roles. However, traditional values are still influential and restraining and our culture remains a context for disrespect and social and emotional irresponsibility.

Some males do, of course contribute to relationships in sensitive, respectful and non abusive ways, in spite of restraining social-cultural influences. An examination of socio-cultural structures and traditions is helpful in understanding restraining influences on males and females as gender groups or as members of various social systems. In order to understand or explain the behaviour of individuals, it is helpful to examine restraining influences at other levels of context.

DEVELOPMENTAL CONTEXT

Males and females practise habits and patterns of relating, in family, school, peer group and other social systems, which either facilitate or impede the development of respectful and sensitive relationships. It is evident that socio-cultural restraints are reflected in families and other social systems. Some family, school and peer contexts reflect these values more strongly than others. Individuals may practice highly restraining relationship habits in highly restraining social systems. Strongly gendered family structures are likely to reinforce restraining ideas for males which promote an exaggerated sense of entitlement, avoidance of social-emotional responsibility and habits of reliance on females for social and emotional requirements.

The confusing evidence regarding family characteristics of abuse perpetrators is more easily understood when viewed in the context of a theory of restraint. Some families are characterized by **"developmental overloads"**, some by **"developmental underloads"** and some by inconsistent or unpredictable mixtures of the two, with respect to the context for facing social and emotional responsibilities.

"Developmental overloads" exist in families where caregivers appear to be insensitive or under-responsive to children's social and emotional requirements. These conditions exist in families where boys are:

---------- physically or sexually abused;

---------- exposed to parental incompetence and neglect;

---------- deprived of sensitive, respectful and nurturing caregiving especially "fathering";

---------- exposed to abusive and disrespectful behaviour in their caregiver's relationship;

---------- expected or allowed to take on inappropriate adult responsibilities in the form of adult work or inappropriate alliances with a parent (e.g. as a parent's companion or confidant).

Such developmental overloads are highly restraining for boys in facing social-emotional responsibilities.

These boys may experience little nurturance, trust, or confirmation and respect of personal boundaries, and witness few of these qualities in their caregiver's relationship. They may not witness respectful ways of handling conflict and conflict resolution skills. They may be required to "grow themselves up" and develop survival or streetwise skills not normally expected of children. Relationship skills best suited to survival are based on competition and defensiveness rather than cooperation, nurturance and trust. Such overloads encourage boys to put energy into traditional male pursuits thus reinforcing socio-cultural restraints. In a context where it is "every man out for himself", boys are likely to practice habits which reflect a sense of entitlement that is out of step with social-emotional responsibility and regard for the welfare of others.

An adolescent who behaves abusively in this context may be subject to excessive, inappropriate and abusive sanctions by caregivers or alternatively no sanctions at all. Abusive behaviour may be ignored, encouraged or even taught in the case of a thirteen year old boy who was physically instructed by his stepfather to sexually abuse his younger sister. Such a context sets a strong precedent for locating the responsibility for abusive behaviour externally and attributing blame to others.

"Developmental underloads" are characteristic in families where caregivers appear to be oversensitive and over-responsive to their children's social and emotional requirements. In such families, boys appear to be excessively reliant on caregivers (generally mothers) to face normal age-appropriate pressures, responsibilities and challenges.

Caregivers appear to excuse boys from responsibilities and apply few meaningful sanctions for irresponsible behaviour. One caregiver may form an alliance with the boy which is characterized by worrying about his welfare but excusing his behaviour. This alliance may exclude the other caregiver who advocates harsher sanctions. Caregivers find themselves increasingly preoccupied with and concerned about their son's development and working harder in their attempts to remind, direct, cajole, advise and influence him to take more responsibility, think more before acting, be more considerate, less selfish and control his temper. The boy, on the other hand, appears to take diminishing amounts of responsibility for these areas of his development and "requires" more and more direction and supervision.

In this context, boys tend to develop a sense of entitlement and self-centredness which far exceeds their sense of responsibility and concern for the welfare of others and other's needs and feelings. Increasingly they avoid taking responsibility for their own actions and develop an excessive reliance on caregivers to worry about and take responsibility for their own social and emotional requirements. Not surprisingly, these boys experience increasing difficulties in handling pressure, disappointment and challenge in relationships. They tend to blame others when things go wrong and experience a diminishing sense of competence.

If boys behave abusively in this context, caregivers are generally concerned but may not act in ways which help the boy to take responsibility for the abuse. Caregivers tend to become preoccupied with the search for an explanation for the abusive behaviour and often look towards themselves, feeling excessive guilt and responsibility. Alternatively

Alan Jenkins

47

they may look for an external explanation which tends to excuse the boy of responsibility. For example, parents of boys who sexually abuse younger children, may refer to their behaviour as experimenting or curiosity and fail to label it as abuse. They unwittingly condone the abusive behaviour in what they believe to be the interests of the boy's welfare.

Many caregivers, in this context, fail to apply meaningful sanctions to abusive behaviour and take increasing amounts of responsibility themselves to try to prevent further occurrences. They worry more and become increasingly vigilant, monitoring their son's temper and behaviour and "walking on egg shells" around him. As they take increasing responsibility, the boy tends to become less vigilant and less likely to monitor or take responsibility for his own actions. Abusive adolescent boys rely on their parents to tolerate and excuse behaviour that is at times grossly abusive and even life-threatening.

Many boys develop habits and values that restrain them from facing social and emotional responsibilities in their **peer context**. They may compete in peer groups which specialise in teasing, bullying or sexual harassment of girls or younger boys. Restraining habits which involve attempts to establish status and power at the expense of other's welfare and feelings, may be rehearsed and practised.

Others may be the victims of teasing, abuse and harassment and develop feelings of social inadequacy and habits of withdrawal and isolation. Some of these boys retreat into a fantasy world in which they become preoccupied with traditional gender stereotyped scenarios of social success and status, dominance, sexual performance and vengeance. Many abuse perpetrators rehearse abusive or exploitative scenarios in fantasy. Sexual offenders may pair this rehearsal with masturbatory behaviour.

These peer contexts promote an avoidance of social and emotional responsibilities, the pursuit of a sense of entitlement at the expense of others' welfare and the attribution of responsibility for abusive behaviour to the victims of abuse.

Some school systems unwittingly promote restraining beliefs by failing to provide appropriate sanctions for abusive behaviour that is perpetrated by students within the school community. They ignore abusive behaviour or attempt to deal with it using conflict resolution techniques that assume equal responsibility for the perpetrator and the victim. Such schools inadvertently promote irresponsible and abusive behaviour by failing to locate responsibility for the abuse with the perpetrator.

Membership of organizations such as the Military or Police Force can provide restraining influences for individual men in facing social and emotional responsibilities (Shupe et al 1987). Such organizations are characterized by rigid hierarchies of "superiors" and "subordinates" and the sanctioning of violence in certain circumstances.

INTERACTIONAL CONTEXT

Some men are able to contribute to respectful and sensitive relationships with their partners and other family members in spite of highly restraining developmental backgrounds. Others, however, live in marriages and families which are characterized by highly restraining patterns of interaction. These patterns of interaction reflect and maintain socio-cultural restraints and developmental habits. Many men maintain a sense of entitlement which is out of step with social and emotional responsibility, as a result of restraining patterns of reliance on their partners or other family members. They fail to "stand on their own feet" and face relationship pressures and responsibilities and consequently can maintain patterns of social and emotional irresponsibility and avoidance.

In a **marital relationship**, patterns of reliance may be based on imbalances in perceived **status and entitlement** or **responsibility** for relationship and family life.

Patterns of reliance, based on imbalances of perceived **status and entitlement** are characteristic of "dominant - submissive" relationships (White 1984). In such relationships, a man may act as a domineering patriarch, propped up by a submissive partner who defers and protects him from any challenge to his authority by any family member. Threats or perceived challenges to the man's authority or sense of entitlement are generally countered with displays of status or power. The man tends to avoid conflict and avoids practicing conflict resolution skills by relying on his partner to defuse conflict. He may attempt to influence or direct aspects of family life but avoids facing social and emotional responsibilities in marriage and family life by relying on his partner and other family members to protect him and do this work for him.

In this context, abusive behaviour is generally associated with displays of power, status and dominance. The spouse abuser may be puzzled by his partner's "disloyal" or "errant" behaviour and may believe that it is his duty to "correct" her. The context of the abuse is one in which he relies heavily on his partner to tolerate, excuse, ignore and forgive his

Alan Jenkins

abusive behaviour. He relies on her to monitor his moods, feelings and his potential for violence and to prevent conflict and violence by defusing risky situations. She is required to accept blame and take responsibility for his emotional state and his abusive actions.

Patterns of reliance may be based on an imbalance in **responsibility** for marriage and family life. In this context, the man may be quiet and passive and takes little initiative for any contribution to marriage or family relationships. He relies on a more active partner to take initiative, orchestrate and organize aspects of family and marital life. (One exception to this pattern of imbalance may be the responsibility for sexual initiative).

When the man's sense of entitlement is threatened or challenged, he tends to withdraw and to avoid conflict and pressure. At this time, he may become preoccupied with fantasies of dominance, sexual conquest or revenge. His partner tends to take increasing initiative to encourage, coach or cajole him into taking more active responsibility in the marriage and family. These attempts are perceived as increasingly threatening by the man and are met with increasing withdrawal. This withdrawal "invites" his partner to further pursue her attempts. What results is a vicious cycle of pursuit and withdrawal.

As a consequence, the man avoids facing social and emotional responsibilities and takes less and less initiative in marriage and family life. Intimacy skills and conflict resolution skills are neglected as he practices dealing with conflict and pressure by withdrawal and avoidance. He may resent his partner's initiatives but remains reliant on her to take responsibility for social and emotional aspects of family and marital life.

In this context, the spouse abuser may come to feel harassed or nagged by his partner and "pushed beyond his limit". He may spend time intoxicating himself with self-righteous and vengeful thoughts prior to abusing his partner. The man may feel dejected and unappreciated and see his partner as "a bottomless pit" whereby "it doesn't matter what I do, I can't satisfy her". He may experience himself as powerless and with no other option and believe that his partner has provoked his abusive actions. In this way, responsibility is attributed to the partner who may herself believe that "she asked for it".

The relationships of most male abusers generally involve a mixture of these two patterns - imbalance in status and responsibility. In spite of their differences, both patterns serve to maintain a sense of entitlement which is out of balance with social and emotional responsibility. Abusive behaviour is seen to be justified when this sense of entitlement is challenged or threatened and responsibility for the abuse is then attributed to an external source, generally the victim. In both patterns, the abuser relies on his partner to face social-emotional pressures and responsibilities for both of them and to take responsibility for monitoring, preventing, tolerating and forgiving abusive behaviour.

Many adolescents who behave abusively maintain an exaggerated sense of entitlement, a pattern of social and emotional avoidance and reliance and a tendency to avoid accepting responsibility for abusive behaviour, as a result of their participation in families which are characterized by restraining patterns of interaction. These patterns have been detailed in the previous section in terms of developmental overloads and underloads.

Both patterns of marital interaction restrain the development of respectful and sensitive **relationships between men and children** in families. The man who relies on his partner to face social and emotional responsibilities, especially those for parenting, may feel:

--------- entitled to regard the children as his property, to expect unquestioned obedience and to impose unrealistic and inappropriate expectations for their behaviour. He may feel entitled to be free of their presence when it is inconvenient or even to use the children for his own purposes - as sexual objects or scapegoats for his own frustrations and problems. This sense of entitlement is evident in the explanations of some sexually abusive males:

She is my daughter and I will do what I like with her;
I wanted her first sexual experience to be good;
I was only teaching her about sex.

--------- entitled "to turn to the children for love and affection", if feeling lonely, unappreciated or unloved. Some child sexual offenders explain their actions:

I loved her too much;
I was only trying to be loving and close to her.

--------- entitled to "turn to" and expect adult partner functions from the children, if a partner is absent, sick or sexually disinterested, dissatisfied or withdrawn. Some sexual offenders explain their behaviour:

Alan Jenkins

My wife wouldn't give me sex, so I turned to my daughter.

Children occupy low status roles and are powerless and highly dependent on caregivers. Hence they have little choice but to defer and are forced to take responsibility for the abusive man's feelings and needs. The man is able to continue to use and rely on a child victim and experiences little challenge to his social and emotional irresponsibility.

Male abusers become increasingly reliant on victims, whether adults or children, to face social and emotional pressures and responsibilities for them and to take responsibility for the abusive behaviour. Abuse is generally perpetrated in a context of exploitation which is gradually developed over time and increasingly extends social-emotional avoidance and reliance, by encouraging the victim to accept more and more responsibility and experience an increasing sense of entrapment.

Abusive men often spend considerable time and energy constructing such a reality for the victim. Abused wives are frequently told they are incompetent, nagging, oversensitive and sexually dysfunctional. Following abusive acts, they may be treated kindly, indulged and promised that they are loved and will not be harmed again. Physically abused children are often told that they are uncontrollable, bad or unlovable. They may be constantly expected to meet unrealistic and unobtainable demands. Sexually abused children are often told that the abuse is normal and in fact an indication of the abuser's love and affection. Sexual abuse is often perpetrated in a context of general neglect and may be the only form of "affection" shown to the child. Sexual abuse perpetrators take advantage of the trust inherent in the caregiver-child relationship and often gradually trick and deceive the child into participation in the abuse. Sexually abused children are often invited to set limits on and even initiate sexual activity. Rewards and privileges may be bestowed in return. The process of constructing a reality for the victim is often evident in the statements of offenders:

She wanted it too;

I would have stopped if she had said she didn't want me to do it;

When she said she'd had enough, I always stopped;

I said to her, 'This is wrong, we must stop it'.

Sexually abused children are often invited to form inappropriate alliances with the abuser in which favors are given and from which the child's mother may be excluded. The child victim may be invited to join in criticizing and berating her mother for her "incompetence". Parent-child boundaries become more and more confused. Secrecy, loyalty and allegiance are reinforced by this reality shaping, isolation from others and the shame and humiliation which the victim experiences. The resulting victim compliance, protection and secrecy, safeguards any challenge to the man's sense of entitlement and his social and emotional irresponsibility. Responsibility for the abuse continues to be located with the victim.

INDIVIDUAL CONTEXT

Socio-cultural, developmental and interactional restraints are reflected in the restraining habits and patterns of thinking of individual abusive men who demonstrate a sense of entitlement which is out of step with social and emotional responsibility. Many of the "characteristics" of abusive men observed by researchers are understandable in this context. These "characteristics", however should not be regarded as fixed personality traits or static aspects of the man's character. They constitute patterns or habits in thinking and behaviour which are seen as inevitable consequences of the man's high levels of social-emotional avoidance and reliance. Men who are practiced at avoiding social and emotional responsibilities are likely to develop restraining patterns of thinking and behaviour which may be described in terms of:

---------- social-emotional "immaturity";

---------- low self-esteem;

---------- self-intoxicating preoccupations and beliefs;

---------- misguided attempts to control abuse.

These patterns reflect restraints at wider levels of context and are further restraining in themselves to men taking responsibility for their actions.

Abusive males demonstrate a high degree of **social-emotional "immaturity"** especially in the context of the family. Many abusive men are quite competent in certain aspects of their life, especially work, but take little responsibility for their own or others' social-emotional requirements or needs. An inevitable consequence of social-emotional avoidance and reliance will be high levels of self-centred and insensitive behaviour and thinking, in certain contexts. The man may "forget" or fail to consider others feelings and take little responsibility for intimacy and conflict resolution. This "immaturity", however, may not be as evident in other less restraining contexts.

Alan Jenkins

Low self-esteem is also characteristic of many abusive males who tend to be highly preoccupied with their own sense of personal competence and adequacy. Low self esteem is not a fixed trait and can be quite dependent on context. Some men, for example, feel competent and adequate in their work but not in their families. Although they may occupy high status roles, many abusers do not feel powerful in aspects of their day to day lives and especially prior to acts of abusive behaviour. In fact, many abusers feel powerless, threatened and impotent and believe that they may be losing control of members of their families or of themselves (Finkelhor, 1983). Traditionally men are expected to be independent and in control of their own lives. However, most abusive men have established a reliance on others to face social and emotional responsibilities and pressures, set limits and prevent abusive behaviour. This reliance on others tends to place control of the man's life in the hands of others and leads to feelings of insecurity and anxiety. Abusive males have often abdicated responsibility for their own sense of well-being and consequently feel somewhat at the mercy of others they rely on.

Many abusive acts are associated with overt displays of status and power and occur in a context where the abuser feels threatened, inadequate or that he is losing control. Alternatively, abusive acts may be associated with covert experiences in which men are preoccupied with fantasies of dominance, idealized admiration and success, sexual performance or vengeance - often in sharp contrast with their real life experience.

Sexual offenders often describe their sexual interest in the child victim in terms of preoccupation with status and interpersonal confidence. They describe themselves as being attracted to the child's size, naivety, vulnerability and deference. When asked about their choice, most describe the child as "easy", available and accessible. Some make statements like, "I felt that I was satisfying her/giving her pleasure", "She was easily satisfied" and that there were "no pressures" and "no demands".

Abusive men are restrained by their own **self intoxicating preoccupations and beliefs**. These ideas are, of course, closely related to their own causal explanations of the abusive behaviour. Spouse abusers often spend considerable periods of time preoccupied with self-righteous thinking and their partner's "injustices" and many sexual offenders show high levels of sexual preoccupation and sexual behaviour of low interpersonal demand. A tendency to "sexualize" needs and feelings associated with status, control, closeness and affirmation, is evident with many sexual offenders, who try to meet many of their emotional requirements with sexual behaviour and initiatives. Sexual offenders tend to have misguided sexual beliefs and fears which relate to traditional mythology about male sexual performance just as spouse abusers may subscribe to misguided beliefs and traditional mythology about anger, conflict and violence in relationships.

Abusive males are generally highly restrained by their own well-intentioned yet unhelpful and **misguided attempts to control their abuse.** These attempts are of course determined to a large extent by the restraining individual theories and explanations of abuse to which the men subscribe. Misguided attempts tend to be based on patterns of avoidance of responsibility for abusive behaviour and patterns of distraction from and avoidance of the abuser's own experience. This is consistent with the tendency to rely on others to take responsibility for the abuse.

Most abusive males fail to attend to their own experience which precedes abusive acts. Spouse abusers often describe themselves as inexplicably and suddenly moving from a calm a state to an abusive state. They spend little time thinking about and noticing the process of self-intoxication as they escalate their own self-righteous thinking, feelings of blame towards their partners and self-justification of violence, prior to acts of violent abuse.

In a similar way, child sexual offenders fail to think about and attend to the process of self-intoxication that accompanies escalating irresponsible sexual preoccupations, plans, fantasies and initiatives.

Most abusive men only think about their abusive actions immediately after an occurrence of abuse. Feelings of guilt, remorse and shame may be felt at such times for short periods. These feelings and experiences are painful and difficult to face. Consequently, they tend to be quickly pushed out of experience and avoided. Justifications, which excuse the abusive behaviour and shift responsibility elsewhere, are soon developed. The abusive male may then quickly "forget" his painful experience. Consequently, he is unlikely to face up to and take responsibility for his actions or to consider their impact upon the victim. In this way, he fails to limit his own abusive behaviour and relies on others to monitor and limit it for him.

Many abusive males try to control their abusive actions by focusing on emotional states which they confuse with the abusive actions themselves. Spouse abusers may believe that to stop violence they must stop feeling angry. Consequently, they try hard to avoid the experience of anger but take little responsibility to cease their violence. In a similar way, sexual offenders may confuse the experience of sexual interest with abusive behaviour. These men try to avoid the experience of sexual interest and to distract themselves from it, in an attempt to control the abusive behaviour. These strategies are invariably unsuccessful and serve to alienate the man from his own experience so that he feels more "under the influence" of his feelings or urges and less likely to take steps to control his actions.

IMPLICATIONS OF A THEORY OF RESTRAINT

I have found causal explanations of abuse, and the search to discover them, to be highly restraining for men in taking responsibility for abusive behaviour and in learning to contribute respectfully and sensitively in their relationships with others. However, causal theories often relate to parameters of cultural structures and traditions, developmental backgrounds, relationship patterns and patterns of individual thinking and behaviour which are helpful in understanding and intervention in abuse, when considered in the context of a theory of restraint. These parameters are seen as restraints to responsibility rather than causes of abusive behaviour. The more restraints that are active, the less likely the man is to take responsibility.

Abuse and exploitation are perpetrated in a context where the man's sense of entitlement overrides his sense of social-emotional responsibility in relation to others. This context exists for a male when he holds highly restrained beliefs and values that foster:

---------- an exaggerated sense of entitlement in relation to others;

---------- the avoidance of social-emotional responsibilities in relationships;

---------- reliance on others to face these responsibilities in relationships;

---------- the attribution of responsibility for abusive behaviour to other persons, events or factors over which he feels he has little influence or control.

His partner may also hold highly restraining beliefs and values which foster:

---------- a sense of female submissiveness or deference in relation to her partner;

---------- a sense of ultimate responsibility for the creation and maintenance of the social-emotional climate in the relationship;

---------- a sense of responsibility for the causation, prevention or consequences of her partner's violence and abuse;

---------- a sense of entrapment or inability to leave the abusive context.

Consequently, patterns of imbalance in perceived status and responsibility between partners often exist in relationships which are characterized by male violence and abuse.

A theory of restraint may be extremely helpful when working with abusive men and members of their families. I work from the assumption that these men do not want to hurt or abuse others and that they do want caring and respectful relationships. Instead of accepting the abuse perpetrator's "invitation" to search for the cause of the abuse, I am able to invite him to consider:

---------- What has stopped him in the past from taking responsibility for his abuse?

---------- What has stopped him from taking responsibility to develop sensitive and respectful relationships with the victim and other family members?

In this way, it remains clear in the therapeutic context, that I regard the abuse perpetrator as responsible for his abusive behaviour. At the same time, I can invite my client to examine restraints to his acceptance of these responsibilities without the risk of unwittingly encouraging him to attribute responsibility to "causal" factors.

The abuse perpetrator can be invited to examine and challenge restraints which range from socio-cultural and developmental traditions and blueprints by which he may have been unwittingly "sucked in " and patterns of interaction whereby he has relied on others to face social and emotional responsibilities and take responsibility for his abusive behaviour, to restraining individual habits, beliefs and misguided attempts to deal with abuse.

I am also able to work with other family members and invite them to challenge restraining patterns of interaction and habits of accepting responsibility for the abusive male's behaviour. In this way, I can address relationship dynamics in families without the risk of attributing responsibility for abusive behaviour to non-abusive family members.

Alan Jenkins

Explanations based on a theory of restraint tend to promote helpful solutions in the form of responsible actions. If the abusive male has failed to take responsibility in these areas:

---------- if he has failed to face up to and accept responsibility for his abusive behaviour;

---------- if he has failed to face social and emotional pressures and responsibilities;

---------- if he has relied on others to face his social and emotional pressures and responsibilities for him;

then the solution is obvious. He must face these pressures and responsibilities himself. A therapeutic strategy can be devised around the concept of responsibility, in which the therapist's role is to decline "invitations" by the abuse perpetrator to attribute responsibility to external factors and invite him to accept responsibility himself.

PART II

THE PROCESS OF ENGAGEMENT OF MEN WHO ABUSE THEIR PARTNERS

"I now know that I hurt you more than I ever realised. It wasn't just the violence. I blamed you for everything that I couldn't hack. I was always right and treated you like shit. I made you carry the can for everything I couldn't face. I took advantage of your love and all the time I was weak enough to think that it was me who was hard done by."

Excerpt from a letter written by an abusive man to his wife, 1990

INTRODUCTION

The abusive man will come to therapy with a story to tell and explanations of his violence and events in his relationship which are quite consistent with his restrained beliefs. He is likely to want to cease his violence. However, he is also likely to be well practised at avoiding responsibility for his actions and attributing this responsibility to external events or factors over which he feels he has little influence. Attempts to address his violence will have tended to involve attempts to invite others to take responsibility on his behalf. These invitations may be thought of in two ways:

---------- **Explicit invitations** to his partner and others to accept his viewpoints, attribute responsibility externally and ignore, excuse, minimise, tolerate, accept blame, be "understanding" or forgive the violence. These invitations are based on expressed expectations and are generally given in the form of direct requests.

---------- **Implicit invitations** to his partner and others to accept responsibility and attend to his violence for him. The man may not be aware of these "invitations" which are implied from his inactivity and failure to take responsible action in the face of his violence. This inactivity provides a somewhat irresistible "invitation" to others who want to influence his behaviour, to step into the void of responsibility in the man's life and try to take action on his behalf.

Others may have attended to his violence by:

- experiencing worry and concern about the violence;
- taking initiative to advise, confront or try to set limits on his behaviour;
- trying to prevent outbursts of his violence;
- trying to remove pressures and challenges from his life;
- trying to calm him down;
- maintaining secrecy about the violence.

Both kinds of invitation may lead others to participate in the problem and perpetuate interactional restraints to responsibility.

Consequently, the man is likely to have well established habits of reliance on others to take initiative, accept responsibility for his violence and work harder than himself to attend to it. There may be a wide circle of others who attend to the violence, including his partner, family members, friends, police, welfare workers and counsellors. Such a cycle of imbalance in responsibility is likely to have escalated over time, whereby the harder others work to attend to the violence, the less responsibility he takes to attend to it himself. In other words, he is likely to have matched the increasing responsibility of others with increasing irresponsibility himself.

In a counselling setting, the abusive man will inevitably approach the therapist with similar explicit invitations to attribute responsibility externally and confirm his restrained views, along with the more implicit "invitations" for the therapist to attend to and take greater responsibility for the violence. The invitations, both explicit and implicit, may be especially pronounced if the man has made the appointment as a result of external pressures or others' initiatives, such as his partner leaving the relationship or presenting him with an ultimatum to attend counselling, or as a result of police, justice system or extended family initiatives.

It is consistent with the long established pattern of mis-attribution and avoidance of responsibility for violence, that others are likely to have taken the responsibility to initiate therapy for the man. Not surprisingly, he may feel distressed and resentful at being coerced to see a therapist and is likely to present in a manner which appears to be highly irresponsible.

In this context, particularly when the therapist is aware of the nature of the abuse, the man's implicit "invitations" for the therapist to take greater responsibility in attending to the violence, can feel somewhat irresistible.

The therapist may be tempted to accept responsibility by:
- directly challenging and confronting the man's explanations;
- giving advice to stop abusive behaviour and engage in more responsible behaviour;
- putting strong arguments against violence;
- trying to "break down his denial";
- criticizing or castigating the client for his behaviour;
- expressing shock and outrage at his actions.

Alan Jenkins

In this way, the therapist may, with the best of intentions, proceed to argue strongly against violence and for responsibility with the man who is in turn "invited" and feels compelled to retell his original story and express his restrained explanations again with greater vigour, intensity and conviction, thus becoming further entrenched in his own unhelpful ideas.

The therapist may find him/herself arguing more and more strongly for responsibility with an increasingly "resistant" client who appears to be taking less and less responsibility for himself.

In trying to avoid such invitations, I have sought ways to invite the man to take responsibility for his own abusive behaviour, and to:

- --------- discover and clarify his own goals in the relationship;
- --------- address his own violence;
- --------- reconsider the issue of responsibility for his violence;
- --------- challenge restraints to accepting responsibility for the violence.

The man is also invited to examine his own blueprint for relating to others and to discover his own capacity for contributing to relationships in respectful and non-abusive ways.

Central to the model is a process of **engagement** which is utilized in all stages of therapy. In this process, the therapist endeavors to act according to the following three principles:

- --------- **Decline** explicit invitations to attribute responsibility for violence to factors beyond the man's influence and implicit "invitations" to take responsibility for the man's violence and attend to it for him.
- --------- **Invite** the man to challenge restraints to acceptance of responsibility for his own actions.
- --------- **Acknowledge and highlight** evidence of the man's acceptance of responsibility for his actions.

The process of engagement is designed to locate responsibility for the man's realizations and achievements within himself, so that he can more readily own and incorporate his capacity for change. In this way, the therapist can facilitate change with "unmotivated" clients and minimise problems with "resistance". This process is in keeping with a major assumption, that only the abusive man himself can change his beliefs and behaviour. The style of questioning used in this approach has been influenced extively by ideas on therapeutic process developed by Michael White (1988).

The following nine steps constitute the model for engagement with abusive and violent men.

- ---------- invite the man to address his violence;
- ---------- invite the man to argue for a non-violent relationship;
- ---------- invite the man to examine his misguided efforts to contribute to the relationship;
- ---------- invite the man to identify time trends in the relationship;
- ---------- invite the man to externalize restraints;
- ---------- deliver irresistible invitations to challenge restraints;
- ---------- invite the man to consider his readiness to take new action;
- ---------- facilitate the planning of new action;
- ---------- facilitate the discovery of new action.

I have found this model to be helpful in helping abusive men to challenge their restraining ideas and patterns of behaviour, enabling them to discover more respectful and sensitive ways of relating with their partners. Abusive men and their partners can challenge unhelpful patterns of attribution of responsibility for violence, thus freeing the men to take responsibility for their own behaviour and both partners to discover more equitable and respectful ways of relating. In particular, the man can take charge of the process of change by making his own arguments for responsibility and discovering his own ways of translating them into new action. The therapist is able to act as a consultant who feeds back information and invites the man to attribute meaning to his behaviour and experience. In this way, the therapist can avoid problems centred around ideas of "resistance" and facilitate the man to discover new directions in his own life.

Alan Jenkins

INVITE THE MAN TO ADDRESS HIS VIOLENCE

I find it helpful to invite the man to address his violence early in the initial contact. This helps challenge issues of secrecy and enables the therapist to decline invitations to ignore, de-emphasize or minimise violence as an issue. The therapist is then less likely to accept responsibility for the man, by inadvertently colluding with his tendency to avoid talking about the violence or to protect him from facing the consequences of his own actions. The issue of violence can be rapidly established as a priority which must be addressed before other issues or problems in the relationship can be faced. Relationship issues and problems are unlikely to be addressed let alone resolved, unless both partners feel safe in expressing their views.

When asked to explain his reasons for attending, the man may be disinclined to acknowledge the existence of his violence. He may attribute responsibility for his attendance to others:

I was told to come;

It was my wife's idea;

I don't know - you tell me.

Alternatively, he may invite the therapist to focus attention on problems other than violence. These may relate to his wife's "unreasonable behaviour":

She can't just walk out after 15 years of marriage;

She's got the problem - she should be here"

or securing her return home or to the marriage;

We argue a lot;

We've got communication problems.

These statements will tend to be accompanied by a tendency to deny or minimise the nature and significance of the violence:

Our problem isn't violence, it's her pushiness;

I'm not a violent man - I don't really hurt her;

I only gave her a tap.

Or to attribute blame to external factors such as marriage problems, work stress, alcohol or his partner's behaviour:

She provoked me;

She doesn't know when enough is enough;

If she wasn't so ... I wouldn't need to hit her.

Many men deny the likelihood of further violence despite an absence of realistic plans for the future:

It won't happen again;

I've made a promise to myself.

The man may acknowledge the existence of his violence but invite the therapist to take responsibility by attributing blame to aspects of his character or personality over which he feels he has little influence:

I've inherited my dad's temper;

I just snapped - I lost control;

I've got a short fuse;

or by presenting in a helpless and pathetic state, begging for advice.

Some men present with invitations and expectations for the therapist to embark on a quest of searching for the elusive "cause" of their violence:

If only I knew why I hit her.

The fruitlessness of such quests for deep underlying reasons has been discussed previously (See Part I).

It is necessary for the therapist to decline these invitations to attribute blame and disregard or minimise violence, in order to talk about "the real problem".

I find it helpful to interrupt the man, if necessary, and ask him to "help me understand" the events which led up to him making an appointment at this time. The therapist can focus on clarification of details of these events, particularly if they include recent episodes of violence. This may include step by step details of who did what, when, where, and how at various points in time. In particular, I am interested in understanding the meanings that the man has attributed to each of these events - the nature of his experience: "What did you think when Jill said ...?" and the meanings he believes that his partner has attributed to each of these events - his perception of his partner's experience: "What did you think Jill thought when you said ...?"

If his wife has left or issued ultimatums following episodes of violence, I am interested in what this has meant to him and how it has affected him, as well as what he thinks her stands have meant to his wife. I decline the invitation to discuss whether or not the violence is justified.

The therapist may invite the man to participate in this discussion and attend to his violence by:

---------- avoiding criticism of his explanations;

---------- apologizing for interruptions and the need to ask so many questions;

---------- explaining the therapist's lack of knowledge about the situation and the need to understand more fully before being able to know how s/he can best help or offer comments;

---------- asking permission to ask further questions about events.

The therapist may discuss the process of the interview with the man by asking, "Can you handle me asking about ...?" This form of asking permission invites the man to take some responsibility for the content of what is discussed and also to challenge himself about his ability to discuss sensitive issues such as incidents of violence.

The therapist should be vigilant, throughout the initial contact, for any evidence of the man's acceptance of responsibility for violence and his attendance at therapy - no matter how small or seemingly trivial. Any such evidence is acknowledged and highlighted by the therapist as evidence of facing up to responsibility. The man is invited to attribute meaning to this evidence. For example, if the man accepts the therapist's invitation to talk about his violence, the therapist may draw his attention to the meaning and significance of the process in which he is engaging:

Are you sure you can handle talking about your violence?

It isn't easy - it takes a lot of courage to face up to the fact that you really hurt someone you love;

How does it effect you to talk about your violence?

He may be invited to contrast his facing up in the session with his behaviour on other occasions or with the behaviour of others and then to notice differences and attribute meaning to new events:

Is this the first time you have talked about your violence and how it really takes you feel, in a honest way with another person?

What does it say about you as a man/your strength/guts, that you are here today and telling me about your violence?

Many men deeply regret hurting their loved ones and want to stop it - but most of them find it too difficult to face up to what they have done - to look

it in the eye so that they can do something about it - let alone come and see
a counsellor;
A lot of men beat around the bush and never find the courage to mention
their violence - many can't handle the feelings that come up inside when they
start to face up and so they cop out instead or try to run away from it;
What do you think it says about you that you are here today?

The man may deny that his initiatives had any thing to do with his attendance. The therapist may respond:

Come on - a lot of men wouldn't come within one mile of this place, no
matter how much they were told or threatened by others - let alone talk about
their violence. I've heard of men who sit out in their cars unable to pluck up
the courage to enter the building.
It must have taken a lot of courage to walk through this door.
You must have felt like shooting through.
How did you succeed here today?

The therapist may express respect for the man's facing up by selecting out and clarifying details of any evidence of responsibility that he shows. By and large, each of the man's attempts to avoid responsibility in the session are interrupted with invitations to face up rather than commented on or challenged directly.

Alan Jenkins

INVITE THE MAN TO ARGUE FOR
A NON-VIOLENT RELATIONSHIP

The man may accept some of the therapist's invitations to notice and attribute meaning to his "facing up" in therapy. He may even notice a difference between his experience in facing up and when he is influenced by his restrained beliefs and explanations. However, he is likely to continue attempts to invite the therapist to minimise violence and attribute responsibility to external factors. The therapist could regard these continued invitations as indications of the man's "true" selfish, uncaring, and malicious nature, and accept the implicit "invitation" to take responsibility and "correct" him. Alternatively, the model of restraint may be called upon to orient the therapist towards different ways of viewing the man's experience and behaviour. In particular, the therapist may invite the man to examine his own goals, with respect to his relationship and his violence.

The man may be regarded as behaving in a way which is totally consistent with restrained beliefs which determine the nature of his efforts; to make sense of his own and his partner's behaviour, to contribute to his relationship, to deal with differences and conflict in the relationship and to control violence. In effect, he is sharing his blueprint for relating and making sense of his own experience with his partner and inviting the therapist to confirm his restrained beliefs. He may regard his partner as unsupportive, uncaring, disloyal, unreasonable, selfish or provocative. He may feel hurt, betrayed or disrespected. He may believe that he is trying to "correct" her or that he is "driven beyond his limit". Consequently, he experiences his violence as "triggered" by her and believes that it will cease only if she changes her ways.

Alternatively, he may believe that it won't happen again because he is now feeling deeply about it, because he doesn't want it to happen again or because it is best to put it behind him and look to the future. He believes that his hopes and good intentions will be sufficient. Consequently, it is not necessary to talk about it.

Implicit in these explanations is a desire for a relationship which is harmonious, loving, caring, respectful and non-violent. Most abusive men that I have met do not want relationships that are characterized by violence and would prefer non-abusive, mutually respectful and caring relationships with their partners. These goals may be contrasted with restrained recipes for relating. Such recipes prescribe attempts to achieve goals and expectations of partners which are unrealistic, misguided and unhelpful.

In his attempts to solve problems in the relationship, the man looks increasingly to his restrained blueprint for relating and tries to make his experience and events fit, only to find his problems escalating. He may experience an increasing sense of impotence and powerlessness at the ineffectiveness of his own efforts as he tries harder to contribute to a respectful and caring relationship using a blueprint which leads only to escalating disrespect, distance and desperation. He may be extremely distressed by his violence and deeply regret his abusive actions. However, his restrained viewpoint prevents him from accepting responsibility and finding effective ways to cease violence. His efforts to help and solve the problem tend to become the problem itself.

I find it helpful at first to invite the man to attend to his goals and desires for his relationship and allow him the opportunity to put forward arguments for a non-violent relationship.

When the man is preoccupied with his partner's "unreasonable" actions and argues that she should be attending therapy, returning home, behaving more loyally etc., the therapist may attend to his desperation and feelings of insecurity as follows:

"I'm hearing one thing loud and clear - it sounds like this marriage is very important to you - it sounds like you don't want to lose it - you don't want Jill to leave".

This approach is illustrated in the following transcript of therapy with a man whose partner who left him following incidents of violence:

Client: *I've got some problems in my marriage - we had a fight and my wife walked out. I tried to get her to come and talk to you ... we've got to face this together ... perhaps you could talk to her ... I can't seem to get through to her.*

Therapist: *Why did your wife leave?*

Client: *I can't understand it ... I know there are some problems but you can't just run away from them.*

Therapist: *What reason did she give for leaving?*

Client: *Well she said it's because I boofed her ... but it's more than that ... everyone has fights ... I dunno, maybe she's on with someone else.*

Therapist: *How did you boof her?*

Client: (angrily) *O.K. I know sometimes I go a bit far ... but that's behind me now. She's been listening to her bloody girlfriend too much.*

Therapist: *How are you hoping I can help you?*

Client: *Talk to her ... get her to come here and see you ... she thinks I've got a problem ... she should be here ... she can't just walk out of twelve years of marriage and the family.*

Therapist: *I guess you've tried pretty hard to convince her to come back?*

Client: *Of course.*

Therapist: *How have you tried to convince her to come back?*

Client: *I've rung her ... sent letters ... I've told her what she's doing to the kids ... I've gone to her parents and told them what she's doing to me and the kids ... I just can't get through to her.*

Therapist: *It sounds like you've tried just about everything you can think of to get her to come back ... and you're getting pretty desperate. This marriage is extremely important to you?*

Client: (tearful) *Of course it is.*

Therapist: *Perhaps the most important thing to you now?*

Client: (nods tearfully)

Therapist: *I know that you want to see if you can get back together with Jill. There are two things I need you to help me understand so I'm properly in the picture. The first thing I need to understand is what kind of marriage you want to have with Jill? The second thing is what kind of marriage you have had in the past?*

The therapist may then ask permission to enquire about the man's goals for his relationship:

Could you help me understand what kind of marriage you want with Jill?

The therapist may ask questions which invite the man to consider new options for his relationship for the first time and to put his own arguments for the kind of relationship that he wants. In this way, the therapist can decline the implicit "invitation" to put arguments for a non-violent relationship and avoid "inviting resistance" from the man, yet still bring the issue of violence into focus:

Do you want your marriage to include violence or do you want a violence-free marriage?

Do you want a marriage in which Jill feels safe with you or frightened of you?

If the man argues for a violence-free marriage, the therapist can invite him to further challenge his restraining views and consider even stronger arguments for responsibility:

Are you sure? Some men think its fair game to bash their wives - some men think its a good way to let off tension, like hitting a punching bag. Some men think that it's what wives are there for - it doesn't matter if someone gets hurt - that's just too bad.

When the man is arguing that his violence will not reoccur, I find it helpful to distinguish between his goals and desire for no further violence and his plans to ensure that these goals are achieved. I can respect his desire and his goals whilst declining to accept his view that violence will not reoccur in the absence of well made plans. He can be invited to consider planning to ensure that he does achieve his goals:

I'm hearing loud and clear that you don't want to use violence again and that you believe you have put it behind you. You seem to be telling me that you don't want a marriage with violence.

Can you help me understand how you came to that decision?

Have you made a decision like it before?

How is different this time?

What sort of plans have you made?

Do you want to quit violence under all circumstances or do you want to hang on to a little for certain occasions?

Would you like to be able to handle any argument without resorting to violence?

Even if you think Jill is totally unreasonable?

Even if you feel provoked?

Are you sure? Some men think that there are certain things a woman deserves to be thumped for. Some men think a wife won't respect a husband who doesn't hit her occasionally.

The therapist may invite the man to consider his goals as they relate to mutual **respect, trust and love** in the relationship:

*Do you want a marriage in which you both feel respected by each other and
satisfied with each other?*

*Do you want a marriage in which you enjoy each other's company or tolerate
each other's company?*

*I understand that you want to stay together but do you want a marriage
where Jill stays with you/comes back to you because she wants to - out of
love and respect or because she feels she has to - out of fear or duty?*

*Are you sure? Some men think that women ought to just do what they are
told - their feelings don't matter.*

*Are you sure its important that she feels love and respect and wants to be
with you? Some men think that it's best to keep a women scared and
chained to the kitchen - to have her fear is better than to have her respect.*

*Would you rather Jill pretend to respect you out of fear or have her genuine
respect and trust?*

The man is also invited to consider the importance and value he
places on these goals:

*How important is it to you to have a marriage based on genuine respect and
trust?*

*How important is it to you to have a marriage in which you both genuinely
want to be with each other?"*

The therapist may respond to the man's arguments for
responsibility by challenging his statements, thus inviting the man to put
stronger arguments for a non-violent relationship. The therapist continues
to decline invitations to attribute blame externally by interrupting, if
necessary and persists in pursuing enquiries about the kind of marriage
the man is really wanting.

Whilst I respect the man's arguments for non-violence and
mutuality, I do not regard them as evidence of his readiness to cease
violence or engage new behaviour. They are regarded as a point of
reference which he has provided and to which the therapist can return
throughout therapy and compare and contrast with the man's actions.

I am not concerned about the "truth" of the arguments - whether
they are true representations of his feelings, socially desirable responses
or attempts to deceive the therapist. I regard them as beginning steps
towards responsibility and integrity and invite the man to entertain these
ideas in a variety of ways. Regardless of initial motivations, I believe that
the man can gradually discover and develop his own integrity and
responsibility, if invited to engage in this process. He is likely to

commence and continue a process of challenging and rejecting previously restraining ideas.

INVITE THE MAN TO EXAMINE HIS MISGUIDED EFFORTS TO CONTRIBUTE TO THE RELATIONSHIP

When the man begins to put arguments for a relationship which is mutually respectful, caring and non-violent, the therapist may invite him to examine ways that he has tried to contribute to such a relationship - his recipe or blueprint for closeness:

I now understand that you don't want to hurt Jill and that you want a relationship where she respects, trusts and stays with you because she wants to and where she feels respected and loved by you. I understand that you want a more respectful and caring relationship. You have made it clear how important this is to you. What I don't yet understand is what has stopped you in the past from achieving your goals.

Do you think it would be helpful if you understood what has stopped you from achieving your goals?

How would this help you?

Could you help me to understand the ways that you have been trying to build this kind of relationship?

Are there times when you feel you have been successful?

What has stopped you or got in the way other times?

How have you tried to solve problems in your relationship?

The therapist can proceed to enquire about the man's perception of the history of achievements and problems and attempts to solve them in his relationship, even if his arguments for non-violent relationship are relatively weak.

The therapist may invite the man to **examine his violence** in this context:

What affect has your violence had on your marriage?

What effect has your violence had on respect/trust/safety/ caring/love in your marriage?

What effect has your violence had on you and how you feel about yourself?

What effect has your violence had on your own self respect/self-confidence?

What effect do you think your violence has had on Jill?
What effect do you think your violence has had on Jill's feelings of trust/respect/love/safety?

The therapist may acknowledge the man's concern and distress about the deterioration which has taken place in his relationship. In this context, the man is invited to describe details of his violence, the context in which it has occurred and its consequences:

Can you help me understand more about your violence, how it has developed and how it has got in the way of your relationship?
Can you handle talking about the last time you were violent to Jill?

The therapist may focus on specific incidents which have included violence and invite the man to recall details of his experience and his perception of his partner's experience, throughout each incident:

What was the first thing that happened?
What did you think when Jill did/said ...?
What did you feel then?
What did you do/say?
What did you want to do?
What did you want her to do?
What do you think she wanted?
What do you think she was thinking/feeling?
What did she do then?
What happened next?

In this way, the therapist invites the man to study the process of his own self-intoxication, in a step by step fashion, throughout each incident. This is a novel experience for many men who tend to see their violence as coming "out of the blue" with no antecedents or build up and who have never considered the way in which they work themselves up to violence. The man is invited to punctuate his experience by reflecting on his thoughts, feelings and actions at significant points throughout each incident.

The man is invited to describe his violence in a specific and detailed manner:

How did you grab her/push her/hit her?
Did you hit her with a closed or open fist?
How many times?
Where did you hit her?

Many men avoid thinking about details of their physical abuse, preferring to keep it out of awareness. Their initial descriptions reflect this avoidance of responsibility:

I gave her a tap;
I got a little physical with her.

Consequently, these questions are challenging and invite the man to "own" his violence and to describe it objectively.

It is vital for the therapist to respond to the man's acceptance of this invitation, by helping him to define his "facing up" as an indicator of strength and courage. This new definition of strength and courage is in marked contrast to the traditional cultural definitions as reflected in movie heroes such as Rambo:

Can you handle talking about your violence up front like this?
How does it make you feel inside to talk about it?
Are you ready to face up to it in this way?
It takes a lot of guts to begin to look it in the eye and talk about the fact that you have done something that has really hurt Jill.
A lot of men run away from it at this point. It's a lot easier to keep it at a distance and not look at it for what it really is.
I have a lot of respect for your courage in facing up to your violence rather than running away from it.
Is this the first time you have talked about details of your violence?
What does it say about you that you can handle talking about your violence?

The man is invited to describe other incidents which have included violence, throughout his marriage and elsewhere and to notice **patterns in the violence and its context.** He is encouraged to notice **patterns in his own experience** and to label this experience in ways which promote acceptance of responsibility rather than attribution to external events. This process is assisted if carried out in the context of examining the contrast between good intentions and misguided actions:

When she complains/disagrees with your point of view/goes out with her friends/wants to do her own thing, how does this affect you? - How does this make you feel about yourself?
Am I hearing you straight? When she ... then you feel hurt/insecure and think that you are losing closeness and respect. You think she is uncaring and disloyal and feel worried about your relationship. Am I understanding you correctly so far?

When you feel worried/insecure/hurt, you then try to put things right by trying to get her to see it your way and trying to get her stop arguing or disagreeing. If she continues - you feel more hurt/insecure/worried and try harder to get her to see it your way. Eventually you resort to desperate methods such as threats and violence.

The thing I'm most aware of is that you are really wanting to be close to her and to respect each other - yet what happens is you wind up hurting her and driving her further away from you.

Can you think of other times when you really wanted to be close to her but ended up hurting her and driving her away/becoming more distant from her?

A man, like the one in the previous transcript, who is desperately pursuing a partner who has left him, may similarly be invited to consider the consequences of his misguided actions and contrast these with his intention to build a mutually respectful relationship. He is initially likely to be quite unaware of the fact that his well-intentioned albeit desperate attempts to solve the problem are, in fact, becoming the problem itself.

INVITE THE MAN TO IDENTIFY TIME TRENDS IN THE RELATIONSHIP

Many abusive men fail to address and to comprehend the nature of the deterioration in their relationships over time. The therapist may assist the man to look beyond his static view of his violence and its consequences, by introducing the dimension of time into questions and examining trends in time in the relationship (White 1986a). In this way he can be invited to attend to the deterioration in his own behaviour and in the relationship:

I understand you are wanting a close respectful relationship. However, have your violence and threats of violence been increasing (in frequency/intensity) or decreasing over the time of your relationship?

Do you think Jill is feeling safer and more relaxed with you or more tense and scared over time?

Do you think Jill is feeling more loving/caring or less loving/caring towards you over time?

Do you think Jill is gaining respect for you or losing respect for you over time?

How do you know this? What does she do/say that tells you this?

Do you think Jill is feeling more respected by you or less respected by you over time?

Have you been feeling more closeness or more distance in your relationship over time?

These trends can be linked with the man's misguided efforts to contribute to his relationship:

How have your attempts to try to get Jill to see things your way affected her over time?

How have your attempts to get Jill to reassure you affected her over time? Are your efforts to try to help the relationship, by giving Jill advice/trying to avoid arguments, leading to more closeness or more distance over time? What effect have your efforts to keep the relationship together, by trying to get Jill to respect your point of view, had on your relationship over time?

Has she become more respectful of your ideas or is she losing respect for them over time?

Are you getting more together or more apart?

How has this affected your chances of having the kind of relationship that you really want?"

The man may be invited to "**collapse time**" (White 1986a):

What will happen if (trend) is continued?

What would it be like in two years time?

If the man's arguments for a non-violent relationship are weak, he can be invited to anticipate the consequences of the continuation of current trends into the future and to contrast his predictions with his goals for the relationship:

What do you think will happen if you continue violence in your relationship?

Do you think Jill will be prepared to hang in there in a violent relationship?

How close is she to leaving for good?

INVITE THE MAN TO EXTERNALISE RESTRAINTS

The therapist may now invite the man to consider explanations for his violence which are based on a theory of restraint, by maintaining a preoccupation with questions that address the following issues. Given his intentions:

---------- What has stopped the man from taking responsibility to contribute to the relationship in ways that foster equity, mutual respect, sensitivity and caring?

---------- What has stopped the man from taking responsibility for his violent behaviour?

In this way, the therapist invites the man to discover and challenge restraining attitudes and habits, in order to free himself to develop the relationship that he really wants.

If the man is preoccupied with the question "Why am I violent?", the therapist may respond:

It never surprises me to hear of violent behaviour like yours. Our culture is riddled with violence and messages about violence. It is impossible to turn on a TV set without seeing examples of violence being used to solve problems or take advantage of others. I am wondering more about what has stopped you from finding ways to develop the kind of relationship you want - one which is not violent but caring and respectful. I am wondering what has stopped you from facing up to, taking responsibility for your violence and putting it behind you for once and for all.

White (1986a, 1989) has described the process of "externalisation" of a problem in order to render a restraining practise or belief accessible to be challenged. In this way the man can separate himself from and pit himself against his own restraining beliefs and practices rather than against his partner or himself.

The man can be invited to externalism his blueprint or recipe for relating and then to examine its relevance to his goals and its implications for his future and the future of his relationship.

When such beliefs are relevant restraints, I generally find it helpful to take the initiative and detail my understanding of the man's blueprint or recipe for relating, in the context of socio-cultural restraints or extended family traditions which reflect patriarchal values.

I prefer to introduce this notion in a somewhat dramatic way:

Therapist: *You know it doesn't surprise me that you have had trouble achieving a loving, respectful relationship and instead got one which is getting further apart and more and more violent. In fact I'm surprised that Jill didn't start to lose her feelings for you before you began the violence.*

Client: *What do you mean?*

Therapist: *Well you wanted to get close to her and you worked hard at it. I respect your intentions. However, your recipe for getting close is not only out of date but totally misguided. In fact - this may come as a shock to you - its probably the best recipe I could think of for insecurity, disrespect and violence in a marriage. Can you handle some straight information about this?*

Client: *Of course I can.*

Therapist: *Your recipe for building a marriage expired years ago and hasn't been renewed. It doesn't match the kind of relationship that you want. It would be a good blueprint if you wanted to be tyrant or if you lived about 100 years ago. It would work well if you wanted a slave, a doormat or a robot rather than a wife - someone who serves you rather than really loves and respects you. However, you were indicating earlier that this isn't want you want. Do you know the old-fashioned recipe for a marriage which says that the man is in the front seat and in charge? He knows best and the woman should be in the back seat doing what she is told and keeping her feelings and thoughts to herself. These old-fashioned ideas say that the man is supposed to be the provider and that his point of view is the correct one and it his duty to help is wife think that way too - for the sake of the marriage. It is easy for men to get sucked in without realising it How much do you think you've been sucked in by these ideas?*

Alan Jenkins

The man is invited to externalize patriarchal restraints and consider their influence in his life and the extent to which he has slavishly and blindly followed a set of oppressive and unhelpful beliefs:

If a man takes this recipe on board what sort of marriage is he going to be building?

Is he going to want his wife to be her own person with her own ideas or his person with his ideas?

Is she likely to respect him more if he tries to get her to be his person or if he allows her to be her own person?

If she was just doing what she is told, would she be more likely to give out of love and desire or out of duty?

The man may also be invited to consider the influence of family traditions which are consistent with these beliefs and the extent to which he has unwittingly followed in the footsteps of another family member.

The man's adherence to this patriarchal blueprint for relating is linked with his failure to achieve his goals, as illustrated in the following sections of edited transcript:

Therapist: *The worst part of it is that you want to get close - that you want your wife's respect and love but you get sucked in to try to make her your person and, of course, she loses respect for you. This out-of-date blueprint says that men should own their wives. So whenever she does her own thing - wants to go out by herself - says her own point of view - disagrees with you, you feel insecure inside and think there is something wrong with her - she's letting you down - she doesn't care, because the old blueprint says she should think the way you think. Then you get sucked in further by the blueprint which tells you to put her right. When she doesn't agree with you, you feel even more insecure and furious with her. Then the blueprint has got you by the balls and you start to resort to desperate methods like threats and violence. The more you give in to your insecure feelings and follow the blueprint, the more you feel trapped in it - and the tragic thing is that you are not wanting to hurt her. You are wanting to get close to her. That's right isn't it?*

Client: (Nodding)

Therapist: *Well it doesn't stop there either. The more you give into insecure feelings - the more you do what the feelings say - the more the feelings start running your life for you.*

They take over the driver seat of your life and you become a slave to them. You become less and less able to think for yourself and less and less able to handle your own life. You start to become more and more reliant on your wife to do your thinking for you and to handle your insecurity for you. You start to need her to put her own life aside and reassure you and prop you up by keeping her mouth shut and not saying or doing anything that she thinks you can't handle. You start to leave it up to her to control your violence for you by walking on eggshells around you. You start to need her to move from the back seat of the marriage into the boot.

Client: (protesting) *I don't think it's got to that.*

Therapist: *I guess she decided to leave rather than have it get to that - it sounds like that's where it was heading. The only way she could have avoided being hit would have been to keep her mouth shut and do what you say. The tragic thing is that it's exactly the opposite to what you have wanted - that's right isn't it?*

The man is invited to consider the "relative influence" of these societal and family traditions and beliefs (White, 1986a, 1989). If he is an unwitting victim of his own loyalty to a traditional blueprint which is depriving him of the relationship he wants, then it will be necessary for him to determine the extent of this tyranny, by searching for any **exceptions** to the rule. The search for exceptions provides a positive focus for the man by orienting him towards discovering his own competence and ability to change rather than reinforcing a sense of incompetence or stuckness:

Have you noticed any times when you have stood up to this old fashioned blueprint?

Have you noticed any times when you have not been sucked in?

Have you noticed any times when you have been able to handle Jill being her own person/speaking her own mind/making her own decisions?

How did you manage that?

Trends in relative influence may then be highlighted:

Are you becoming more able to make your own decisions in your marriage or more sucked in by these old traditions?

Are you learning to handle and respect Jill being her own person more or are you needing her to be your person more and more over time?

Alan Jenkins

The man is asked to search for and cite evidence which supports his answers to these questions and then attribute meaning to this evidence:

How have you been able to break away from old habits and traditions?
What does this say about you as a person?
What will it mean for you/your relationship if you continue in this direction?

EXTERNALISING "OPPRESSIVE" FEELINGS

I find it helpful to externalize feelings or experiences which are associated with the man's violent actions. Feelings such as "hurt", "insecurity", "frustration", "fear", "impatience" may be usefully externalized. I avoid encouraging men to externalize experiences and feelings such as "aggression", "violence" and "temper" in case the man becomes confused and thinks that the therapist is suggesting that he is not responsible for his violent or aggressive behaviour. When externalising feelings and experiences, I tend to focus on feeling states which the man may not have previously identified and which when labelled invite consideration of new directions and solutions to problems, other than violence.

The man may be invited to consider the relative influence of such feelings or experiences:

Can you think of a time when you felt insecure/hurt and you didn't let it take you over?
Can you think of a time when you stood up to your hurt feelings and didn't let them push you around?
How did you do it?

For some men, their childhood experiences may have fostered habits of being driven by feelings of hurt and insecurity. These habits may still be practised years later. Trends in relative influence over time, may be examined:

Are you becoming more or less sucked in by your hurt/insecure feelings over time?
Are you using your head more when you are angry or losing it more over time?
Is your insecurity getting you tighter and tighter in its grip over time or are you finding ways to stand up to it?
Are you starting to find ways to steer your life or is your insecurity taking over the wheel more and more over time?

EXTERNALISING PATTERNS OF RELIANCE AND AVOIDANCE OF RESPONSIBILITY

Habits of avoidance of responsibility by the male and reliance on his partner to take responsibility for violence, may be usefully externalized (for both partners), particularly when inviting the man to consider the question:

What has stopped you from taking responsibility for your violence?

The man may first be invited to consider who has **attended** most to violence in the past:

Who has tended to think/worry most about your violence in the past?

Who thinks most about the violence after the event?

Who thinks most about the risk of violence before the event?

Who has studied/been on the look out/tried to monitor your violence, the most?

How have you both tried to live with violence?

How has your partner tried to live with violence?

What has she needed to do?

How have each of you tried to control or stop violence in the past?

Who has worked hardest to try to control or prevent violence in the past?

Whose job has it been seen to be?

Who has worked hardest to put the brakes on and prevent violence? How?

Who is most likely to back down/walk away in arguments if there is a risk of violence?

Who has had most practise at putting the brakes on?

Have you worked harder at trying to find ways yourself or harder at trying to get your partner to put the brakes on?

What would happen if you continued in this way?

What would happen if you continued to rely on your partner to control/prevent violence?

Would you feel that you were loosing or gaining control of yourself over time?

What would it mean for you/your partner/your relationship?

The therapist may draw the man's attention to traditional and old fashioned blueprints regarding the **responsibilities of men and women in marriage**:

Are you familiar with the old fashioned recipes for what is regarded as men's work and women's work? Men were seen to have no other responsibility in the family than to be providers of material things. Women, on the other hand, were seen as having the job of looking after everyone's feelings in the family and making sure that everything ran smoothly and that there was no conflict or bad feelings. If anyone felt insecure, upset or unhappy, then it was her job to look after them, calm them down or prop them up. It was her fault if somebody else felt upset and her job to make them feel secure again - to prop them up by pretending that it was her responsibility and accepting blame for whatever went wrong.

What would happen in a marriage in which both the man and women were completely sucked in by these blueprints?

Would the man get stronger and more able to stand on his own feet and handle his own pressure or would he get weaker over time?

Would he become more independent over time or more reliant on his partner when things don't go the way he wants?

Would he be more needy of his partners protection and propping up or more able to prop himself up over time?

The man may be invited to examine his own **theories of violence** in this context and to consider the extent to which they have either helped or hindered him in achieving his goals. It is generally helpful to invite the man to examine his theories based on notions of **provocation**:

If a man sees his violence is caused by another person what does this mean in terms of his ability to be able to control it?

Who would he come to rely on to control it - himself or his partner? Would he come to need a wife or a minder over time?

What would it mean for his ability to be able to handle pressure both at home and work?

Who would he feel was running his life - himself or his partner?

How would this affect his feelings about himself - would he feel more capable or more incapable over time?

If a man relied on his wife to calm him down when he was upset by pretending to agree with him or to humour him - what would this mean for his ability to handle tough situations and to face pressures both at work and home in the future?

The man who sees himself as "snapping" or **"losing control"** may be invited to understand that he does in fact exercise control, even during violent outbursts. The following transcript of therapy illustrates this invitation.

Client: *I snapped when she kept on at me - I just lost control - I couldn't help myself - I laid into her and kept thumping her.*

Therapist: *Did you use a weapon - perhaps a knife - did you stab her?*

Client: (Looking startled) *Of course not.*

Therapist: *Why not - what stopped you from killing her?*

Client: *I'd never attack her with a knife - only my hands*

Therapist: *You chose not to use a weapon then. Did you knock her unconscious or break her arm?*

Client: *No way.*

Therapist: *How did you stop yourself then?*

The therapist can then invite the man to consider the consequences of failing to attend to his own violence and his own self-intoxication and the way that this failure to take responsibility contributes to his experience of loss of control.

Once again, the man is invited to consider the relative influence of these restraining ideas and practices and especially to identify instances of self-reliance:

Can you remember a time when you took action to stop/prevent violence yourself?

Can you remember a time when you made a stand against your own violence and did not expect your partner to do it for you?

How did you do it?

The man is also invited to consider trends in relative influence regarding this reliance on his partner:

Are you becoming more reliant on Jill or more self-reliant over time - for control of violence? - to face your pressures/calm you down?

He is encouraged to notice evidence which supports new trends in self-reliance and to attribute meaning to this evidence:

How did you manage to stand on your own two feet and avoid dumping your problems onto Jill?

What does this say about you?

What will it mean for your future/the future of your relationship?

Alan Jenkins

DELIVER "IRRESISTIBLE INVITATIONS" TO CHALLENGE RESTRAINTS

Once the man has begun to externalize restraints and consider their influence in his life, he can be invited to challenge these restraining ideas and habits. These invitations can be quite confronting and highlight a personal challenge which the man may find somewhat irresistible. In this way, he is invited to make his own commitment to self-responsibility and mutuality in his relationship.

RESPONSIBILITY FOR VIOLENCE

Could you handle a marriage in which you control your own violence, or do you need Jill to try to control it for you by keeping her mouth shut/walking on eggshells around you?
Do you want to take action to put the brakes on yourself or would you be prepared to leave it to Jill to continue to try to put the brakes on for you?
Are you sure? It won't be easy - you've had little practice in setting limits for yourself. It would be a lot easier to leave it up to her?
Even if you feel she's unreasonable or provocative?

NON-OWNERSHIP

Could you handle a marriage in which Jill says what she really thinks, or do you need her to look after your feelings by saying what she thinks you want to hear?
Could you handle a marriage in which Jill is her own person and speaks her own mind, or do you need her to pretend to be your person?
Could you handle sharing the front seat of your marriage with Jill, or do you need her to prop you up/support you by staying in the back seat?
Are you sure? What if she disagrees with you or has different opinions?

SELF-RESPONSIBILITY FOR FEELINGS

Are you wanting to stand up to the influence of your feelings of insecurity/hurt/jealousy and take charge of your own life, or would you be prepared to continue to surrender to them and let them have their way with you/to continue to feel pushed around by these feelings?

Could you handle a marriage in which you stand on your own two feet and face pressures when they arise, or do you need to lean on Jill by getting her to look after your feelings for you/to calm you down?

Could you handle a marriage in which you stand on your own two feet and face your own pressures or do you need Jill's protection by having her to face your pressures for you?

Could you handle a marriage in which you look after your own feelings and find your own security or do you need Jill to prop you up and try to make you feel secure?

Are you sure? It's a lot easier to rely on her to save you from pressure and face your pressures for you?

OLD TRADITIONS

Could you handle the pressure of leaving the old fashioned blueprint about men and marriage behind and deciding your own future for yourself?

Do you think you could handle the pressures of your friends/parents etc. and still make your own decisions or do you see yourself getting sucked back in by their pressure?

Wouldn't it be easier to change your goals about the kind of marriage you want than try to change your recipe about how to go about getting it?

TRUST AND RESPECT

Is it important for you to try to earn back Jill's respect and trust or do you think she should give it out of duty?

Is it important for you to earn genuine trust and respect or would you settle for a pretence - Jill just saying what she thinks you want to hear?

How important is it for you to try and earn it back or would you settle for trying to: - beg for it back? - buy it back? - demand it back? - con it back?

Alan Jenkins

INVITE THE MAN TO CONSIDER HIS
READINESS TO TAKE NEW ACTION

When the man is arguing for self-responsibility, self-reliance and non-violence, he may be invited to consider his readiness to translate these arguments into action.

At this point, he may be keen to pursue his partner and try to convince her that he is a changed man. If she has considered leaving him, he may want to try to convince her to stay. If she has left him, he may want to convince her to return. These tendencies are, of course, indications of the perseverance of old restraining habits, not readiness for new action.

Rather than discuss how he can convince or prove himself to his partner, the man is invited to consider how he can **prove to himself** that he is ready to quit being dominated by old habits and blueprints and that he is ready to contribute to a mutually, respectful and non-violent relationship. The therapist may comment:

Lots of men at this stage are keen to jump in and try to convince their partners that they have changed before they have had the opportunity to prove anything to themselves. If you tried to convince Jill before you had proved you could stand up to the old habits yourself.

What would this say to you/to Jill?

Would it be you talking or your insecurity/desperation talking?

Would Jill be likely to be convinced or more likely to think she's heard it all before?

Are you ready to start taking action to prove to yourself that you are ready for a new respectful and non-violent relationship?

Are you ready to start taking action to prove to yourself that

- Jill is safe from violence and threats of violence under any circumstances?

- you can take your own action to prevent violence?

- you don't need her to put the brakes on for you?

- you can stand up to your feelings of ...?

- you don't want to own her?

- you can respect her rights and handle her being her own person?
- you can handle her speaking her own mind?
- you don't need her to look after your feelings/prop you up?
- you can stand up to the old blueprint?
What makes you think you're ready?
What evidence is there that you are ready?
What makes you think you can handle a relationship where your wife speaks her own mind?
Are you sure?
You've practised these old habits for years.
You've been a slave to them for a long time.
Old habits die pretty hard.

The therapist may highlight the significance of departures from old and oppressive habits by pointing out the **strength and courage** that will be required to make such a stand:

It will take a lot of courage and determination to resist being sucked back in by old habits that have pushed you around for many years. Do you think you have the strength to face up to it now?

The man's initial arguments for his own readiness to take action may be facile and ill-founded. It is helpful for the therapist to invite him to challenge the grounds for his readiness and give more consideration to what he is up against. The following dialogue is part of a transcript of an interview with a man whose partner left him following a violent outburst. He has previously acknowledged the influence of his fears and insecurity which he experienced when his partner made her own independent decisions.

Therapist: *You've made it clear you want a marriage where your wife can be her own person - where you don't try to own her. Are you ready to start checking out whether you can handle this kind of marriage?*

Client: *Yeah, if she comes back things will be really different.*

Therapist: *Hang on. She'd be nuts to come back unless she saw some evidence that you could handle her making her own decisions. Would you come back if you were her - with just a promise to go on? If you contacted her tonight and told her things will be different from now on, what effect would it have? Do you think she would be likely to believe you or more likely to think I've heard all this before?*

Alan Jenkins

Client: *Yeah, but how can I prove to her I've changed if she doesn't come home?*

Therapist: *Before you prove anything to her, won't you need to prove to yourself that you can respect her feelings? What is it that she is wanting from you now? What does her not returning your calls tell you?*

Client: *She says she wants time to think. She says she wants time to herself. She keeps saying she is not ready but ...*

Therapist: *What would you be doing then if you were respecting her feelings and wishes now?*

Client: *But I'd give her time to think if she came home.*

Therapist: *It will probably be the hardest thing you've ever done - to prove to yourself that you can respect her feelings and decisions - to prove that you are bigger than your fears and your desperation which I bet even right now are telling you call her and try and convince her to come home. How important is it that you stand on your own two feet and make this decision for yourself? Or are you prepared to let your fears and desperation decide it for you?*

Client: *I want to make the decision - but couldn't I just see her and talk to her.*

Therapist: *Until you've proven you can stand up to your fears and desperation she'd be crazy to talk to you about coming back. Until you've proved to yourself that you can't be pushed around by your insecure feelings, you'd be kidding yourself if you thought you were ready to see her.*

Client: *I can't handle not seeing her - not hearing from her - not knowing how she is...*

Therapist: *Like I said, this will probably be the hardest thing you've ever attempted. Your fears and your desperation are going to be at you all the time telling you to contact her, drive past her house, ring her parents. I can understand if you are not ready to make a stand at this time - if you're not ready to handle it yet. Do you want me to continue?*

Client: *Yes. I want to try it.*

Therapist: *What would it say about you if you stopped trying to make contact with her - if you left it for her to make contact with you when she's ready? What would you be proving to yourself?*

Client: *I guess that I could give her time - that I can handle it.*

Therapist: *Which side of you would it strengthen - the side of you that wants to be able to stand on your own two feet and stand up to your fears - or the side of you that needs her to reassure you?*

Client: *Standing on my own two feet.*

Therapist: *What message would it give to Jill about you, if you stop trying to make contact with her? Do you think she would feel more respected if you stopped or more respected if you kept up trying to make contact?*

Client: *I guess she would feel respected - but if I don't contact her, she might think I don't want her back.*

Therapist: *Is that you talking or your fears and desperation talking? Think about what's happened over the last two weeks.*

Client: *I suppose it's my fears.*

Therapist: *Its going to be pretty tough. You've been pushed around by your fears for years and they're not going to let up easily. In fact its going to feel almost impossible to resist them at times. They will come up with what seem to be excellent reasons for making contact with her and try to pull the wool over your eyes. Do you think you're ready to make a stand against them?*

Client: *Yes, I'm ready.*

Therapist: *Okay, are you ready to make some plans so that you are prepared for them?*

FACILITATE THE PLANNING
OF NEW ACTION

The man who argues for his own readiness may be invited to invent ways of translating his resolve into plans for new action. These plans mays relate to a variety of themes.

PROMOTING SAFETY AND NON-VIOLENCE

The first priority for the man is the cessation of violence and harassment and the promotion of a safe environment for his partner. I decline to discuss any other issues relating to the marriage until the man has developed and begun to act on clear and realistic plans for taking responsibility for his violent behaviour.

The man is invited to contribute to his partner's safety by inventing active ways to demonstrate to himself and to her that he is a safe person to be with:

What would you need to do to get violence/abuse out of your marriage (and your family) once and for all?

How could you prove to yourself and others that you can take responsibility yourself to prevent violence?

Initially he may only consider passive strategies which require him not to take action. e.g. "I won't hit her again." He may instead, be invited to consider **active strategies** which require that he takes new action.

For example, he may be encouraged to **chart his experience** when he feels tense, angry, insecure or experiences other feelings which have been associated with his violence in the past:

Would it be more helpful for you or your partner to study your feelings and what is happening inside you when you are angry?

Pro-formas for recording this experience such as "anger-logs" may be helpful (Gondolf 1985). The man may be encouraged to chart his own habits of self-intoxication with anger and self-righteousness and to discover his own "**red-line**" or point which when reached signals danger and the need to set limits on thinking and behaviour.

He is encouraged to notice and record characteristic recurring feelings, experiences and thoughts which can help him to identify this "red-line" in future events. In this way, he may discover helpful cues to take action early in the cycle of self-intoxication:

What would be the best point to take action to put the brakes on in an argument?

What signs will tell you that it is time to exit from the argument?

Strategies such as "**time out**" may be helpful in this context (Gondolf 1985):

Would it be more helpful if you took action to put the brakes on when you are angry with Jill or if you left it up to Jill to put the brakes on?

The man is encouraged to understand the difference between "time out" and "copping out". "Time out" requires a pre-arranged plan with his partner whereby at any early warning sign of risk of violence, he will signal that he is physically separating himself from her, in order to take responsibility for his own behaviour and calm himself. When he is calm, he returns to his partner to make contact with her again and explain his feelings and actions.

When practising strategies such as "time out", the man is encouraged to prepare himself and plan for unexpected behaviour by his partner. She may not at first understand the nature of "time out" and think that is a new method of intimidation or simply another instance of avoidance of responsibility. She may in fact pursue him and demand that he stays and talks to her.

The Therapist may invite the man to invent his own methods to promote safety:

What could you do to demonstrate to yourself and to Jill (and your kids) that you put safety first?

How could you prove to yourself and to them that they are safe from violence and abuse, no matter what they say or do?

How could you prove to yourself and to them that no matter how hurt or angry you feel, you can handle let downs, differences or arguments without resorting to violence or abuse?

How would you know if anyone in the family was feeling scared of you?

What would you need to do to reassure them that they are safe?

Alan Jenkins

The man who tries to promote safety is likely, at first, to experience self-righteous anger and may feel that his partner is not showing sufficient appreciation of his efforts to stop violence, particularly when he uses strategies such as "time out". He will have relied heavily on his partner's support in the past and, in a dependent manner, may expect her to lavish praise on him for his good efforts. The therapist should predict the likelihood of self-righteous anger and help the man to understand that his partner will naturally be suspicious of his new behaviour at first. Following a period of skepticism she may feel safe enough to speak her mind a little more or raise issues of difference or disagreement. Consequently, she may appear to be critical rather than grateful. The man is encouraged not to misinterpret her behaviour as evidence of a lack of goodwill on his partner's behalf. It is best regarded as an indication that he has been successful in setting conditions to enable his partner to feel safe enough to speak openly to him. It means that his efforts are successful and are being noticed and taken seriously by her. He can now be faced with the dilemma as to whether or not he is ready to understand and handle behaviour which at times seem provocative and unreasonable, without resorting to violence. An opportunity is also provided for the man to demonstrate sensitivity to his partner's needs and feelings.

PROMOTING SELF-RESPONSIBILITY

The man may be invited to invent active ways in which he can demonstrate to himself that he can take responsibility for his own feelings and behaviour. These may involve "plans and strategies" to resist the influence of feelings such as insecurity, fear, impatience etc.:

What would you need to do to prove to yourself:
- that you can stand up to your feelings of ...?
- that you are not a slave to your feelings of ...?
- that you are bigger than your feelings of ...?
- that you can handle feeling hurt/let down/angry without taking it out on Jill?
- that you can stand on your own two feet and you don't need Jill to look after/coddle your feelings for you?
How would you know if you were starting to feel ...?
What warnings signs would you pick up in yourself?
What would you need to do to become more sensitive to these warning signs?

What could you do to take responsibility when you pick these warning signs?
What could you do to help Jill to resign from being the monitor of your feelings?
How could you convince both yourself and Jill:
- that you don't need her to be so vigilant;
- that you don't need her to put the brakes on;
- that you don't need her to calm you down when you get upset;
- that you will take over this job yourself?
Would it be more helpful to make contact or to keep your distance from Jill when you feel insecure?
Which option would help you to stand on your own two feet/find your own security?
Would it be more helpful to talk about your feelings or stew about them?
Who would you talk to?
How will your feelings of ... try to suck you back into old habits of relying on Jill or taking it out on Jill?
How will your feelings of ... try to pull the wool over your eyes and lead you back into old habits?
What could you do to increase your vigilance/prepare yourself?

DEMONSTRATING RESPECT AND NON-OWNERSHIP

The man may be invited to invent active ways to demonstrate respect for his partner's rights, feelings, ideas and independence:
What would you need to do to prove to yourself that you don't need to try to own Jill?
How could you show both yourself and Jill that:
- you can respect her being her own person with her own opinions and ideas?

- that you can respect her independence?
- that you are interested in her opinions whether you agree with them or not?
- that you can handle and want her to share the front seat of your relationship rather than stay in the back seat?
- that you want to share responsibility for your marriage and family rather than rely on her to take all responsibility?

The man is encouraged to monitor and attribute meaning to his actions each time he has contact with his partner. Each of his actions gives either a message of respect or disrespect regarding his partner's rights. He

Alan Jenkins

may be encouraged to keep an inventory or balance sheet of evidence of respect and disrespect. This inventory can be used to measure the direction and strength of trends in his behaviour and prevents him from relying solely on subjective impressions and feelings. The man who is separated from his partner, of course, communicates respect by keeping his distance and observing her right to privacy.

Once again he is encouraged to anticipate the oppressive influence of old habits:

What will be the toughest tests of your resolve to prove that you don't want to own her?

What kind of situations have most easily sucked you into old habits in the past?

In what kind of situations are you most likely to think that:

- you are right and she is wrong?

- you are more entitled than she is?

- she can't say/do that?

What feelings will be most likely to get in the way?

How will you prepare yourself for these?

What if you think your wife is being really unreasonable? How will you handle it then?

The man whose partner has left him may be invited to find ways to resist the tendency to pursue her:

How will your fears/insecurity try to pull the wool over your eyes and convince you that it will be OK to contact her just once or drive past her house?

How will you pick this when it starts to happen?

What will you do then?

Who could you call instead?

What could you do instead?

The man is encouraged to spend time facing his insecure feelings rather than feeling frightened of them, trying to run away from them or distracting himself from them. He is encouraged to practise challenging their influence and thereby strengthening his own influence in his own life.

Active strategies, in this context, may also involve the development of support networks, which do not include his partner, for emotional support and reassurance. New recreational and social activities may be planned to facilitate independence and challenge passive habits of inactivity such as sitting by the phone and waiting for his partner to call.

DEMONSTRATING RESPONSIBILITY FOR PAST ABUSIVE BEHAVIOUR

The man is invited to find active ways to demonstrate his responsibility for his past violence and abuse:

What would you need to do to convince yourself and your partner that you accept full responsibility for your past violence and abuse?

One such active strategy involves finding ways to respect his partner's privacy and space and her decision to separate:

Would it more helpful to you and to Jill, to let her make contact or for you to try to make contact?

If you kept your distance, what message would this give Jill about who is taking responsibility?

If Jill makes contact with you, how could you convince her that you understand and respect her need for space/separateness?

It is almost irresistible for some men to be "sucked in" to trying to make plans for the future, asking for reassurance and telling their partners how much they love them, when the partners make contact. This urge may be anticipated and planned for by asking:

How could you get sucked back in to old habits when trying to let Jill know that you respect her need for separateness?

What things would you need to avoid doing to keep it a message about responsibility?

How could you unwittingly turn it into:

- a guilt trip?

- an argument?

- pressure to reunite?

When a couple separates, following violent incidents, it is often the woman (and children) who leave the family home. The man may be invited to consider which kind of living arrangement would best demonstrate respect and responsibility to his partner.

Do you think it would be more appropriate/fair if you were living in the house or if your wife (and kids) were living in the house?

If you moved out, what would that say about your readiness to take responsibility and bear the consequences of your abuse?

Alan Jenkins

At an appropriate point in therapy (usually when the man has a sense of achievement and influence over his actions), he may be invited to examine more closely the real nature and extent of his violence, abuse and harassment and their **impact** upon his partner and others in the family. This involves a shift from looking inwards at his own experience, to considering his partner's (and other's) experience and developing and **demonstrating sensitivity and understanding** of what he has put others through. This step from introspection or "looking in" to "looking out" often proceeds a new stage of understanding and sensitivity towards his partner's feelings and experience.

Having acknowledged and highlighted certain of the man's achievements, the therapist may enquire:

Are you ready to take a new step which will be a lot tougher than anything you have tried to do so far?

Are you ready to take a closer look at the past - at what you have put Jill (and the kids) through - at what it would have felt like to be in their shoes?

The therapist may challenge the man's resolve with irresistible invitations:

Can you handle a step like this? It means facing up fully to what you have done and trying to understand what it has meant to Jill (and the kids). I know that some men, once they feel they have stopped their violence, think that it can now be forgotten - they can pretend it never happened and expect their partners to do the same, even though their partners are still carrying painful mental scars and memories of the abuse.

On the other hand, others feel they have a responsibility to help with the healing of these scars and memories by trying to understand as best they can what they put their partners through, so that when the time is right they can let their partners know this and make a genuine apology - not one of the pretend ones they made in the past.

Where do you stand on this?

If the man argues for facing up then the therapist may challenge his resolve even further:

It is a pretty painful step to take. It will make you feel pretty horrible at first. It means facing feelings of shame, embarrassment, and grief - if you really let yourself feel about what you have put them through. Yet it's the only way you can make a genuine apology.

Do you think an apology would mean anything at all if you had no idea what is was like for them?

What message would it give Jill, if you tried to apologise without having any idea what it was like for her?
What would it say about you?

The therapist may promote a definition of strength that is gained through facing up to a difficult challenge and painful feelings:
Do you think it would make you stronger or weaker to really face up in this way?
What would it say about you as a man?

The feeling of inner strength is seen to follow behind the painful experience which accompanies facing up, just as the experience of fitness lags behind the pain and discomfort experienced in physical exercise.

If the man demonstrates readiness for facing up then the therapist may assist by prescribing written assignments (e.g. writing "Jill's story") or by asking specific questions, like the following:
What would it be like to be constantly living in fear of violence if you open your mouth?
What would it be like to be constantly on the lookout and worrying about your partner's moods?
What would it be like to be called ... and to be humiliated in front of your family?
What would it be like to be treated like a nothing, as though your opinions didn't matter?

It may be appropriate for the man to let his partner know what he has realised about his actions and their impact on her and others, in the form of an apology. The apology is regarded as a declaration of acceptance of responsibility and distinguished from any previous pleas for forgiveness. It is a gift of understanding and realization which is given to the partner, with no expectation of or request for a response let alone forgiveness, reunion or any change in the partner's behaviour. It is simply a statement of the man's realizations about his abusive behaviour and its impact on others. An apology is totally inappropriate and can even be disrespectful in the absence of genuine attempts to understand the experience of those victimized by the abuse.

This kind of facing up can help the man to understand that his partner's fears and concerns will remain for some time after he has ceased his violence and that it will take considerable time and evidence fore him to earn her trust back, if she ever fully trusts him again.

Alan Jenkins

FACILITATE THE DISCOVERY OF NEW ACTION

Throughout therapy, the therapist endeavors to discover and highlight evidence of the man attempting to stand up to restraining habits and ideas. Examples of these attempts are solicited and then discussed, examined in detail and contrasted with old practices.

Frequently, men fail to notice their own departures from old habits and remain preoccupied with perceived failures in other areas. The man is invited first to notice and then to attribute meaning to these events. The therapist may respond in somewhat dramatic ways to draw attention to achievements and help the man to notice them. (White,1986a).

For example, a man who resists the tendency to pursue his partner after having harassed her for a period of time, may be responded to with surprise or even shock:

You didn't ring her or try to visit her once!!!? How did you do it?

Did you get a friend to check up on her?

Were you sick?

Was she away on holidays?

You have been a slave to your insecure feelings for years. How did you stand up to them?

How did they try to pull the wool over your eyes?

How did you manage to see it like it really is?

What does this step tell you about yourself?

What does it tell you about your own strength and the direction that you are heading in?

I do not find it helpful to praise the man for his achievements. This only tends to encourage dependency on the therapist's opinion to evaluate his behaviour or rejection of a compliment. It is more helpful to invite the man to notice his own achievements and attribute his own meaning to them in terms of his personal goals and those of his relationship.

COUPLE THERAPY

The initial therapeutic engagement of the man is generally carried out in an individual therapy setting, whether he is living with or separate from his partner. If violence is an identified problem, I find individual therapy with the man to be helpful in emphasizing his responsibility for the violence and encouraging him to "stand on his own two feet", even if both partners are keen to engage in couple therapy. Once the man is putting forward some argument for responsibility for his violence (generally after one or two sessions), it may be appropriate to invite him to join a men's group and/or to see him with his partner, if the couple are living together or both desire to reunite.

The men's group has advantages in addressing violence because its gender-based composition emphasizes that men are responsible for their violence and that men can help one another to cease it rather than rely on their partners. Partners do not attend the group and consequently the control of violence is not seen as their responsibility. Appropriately timed couple work can be invaluable in conjunction with a men's group or on it's own. The therapist can then be sensitive to the woman's needs and can understand and help her to clarify her goals with respect to the relationship. Levels of safety in the relationship can be monitored and the therapist can compare and contrast the man's perceptions of events with those of his partner.

Partners can also be helped to understand the major principles of therapy with domestic violence. In particular, the priority of addressing violence first and the tenet that the man is fully responsible for his own violence are important for the woman to understand and may help alleviate her tendency to feel responsibility. Women partners can also be helped to understand the aims and practices designed to promote responsibility, that are employed in the men's group. This can help prevent the confusion and misunderstanding which sometimes occurs when partners first encounter new ideas such as "time out". Most importantly, the therapist can address any of the woman's restraining beliefs and

Alan Jenkins

practices which foster the man's pattern of reliance on her to take responsibility for his violence. In this way, the therapist may more effectively help disrupt interactional restraints.

The woman may be invited to consider how she can take responsibility for her own safety but decline taking responsibility for her partner's violence. She may be encouraged to develop a sense of entitlement to her own rights, independence and safety from violence and intimidation. She may be helped to discover new ways of evaluating her partner's actions which are based on objective evidence rather than obligation, hope or wishful thinking.

The therapist may clarify some of these issues in an individual appointment with the woman before establishing a joint appointment, particularly in view of the fact that she may feel intimidated and unable to talk freely in the presence of her partner. At the least, the man's permission should be sought for the therapist to make contact with his partner by phone. I believe that the therapist has a responsibility, not just to consider the needs of the male client but also to ensure that therapy is sensitive to the needs of those victimized by his abusive behaviour. The following discussion of couple therapy focusses specifically on the engagement of abusive men in a couple context. It does not intend to cover all issues relevant for working with abused women.

In couple work, as in individual therapy, the therapist may invite both partners to focus on the issue of violence and the man to accept responsibility for his violence and challenge restraints to responsibility. In couple therapy, there is an additional focus. The woman is invited to decline accepting any responsibility for her partner's violence and to challenge restraints to taking responsibility for herself and her own actions, as opposed to those of her partner.

The woman may come to therapy feeling afraid to talk openly and honestly about her partner's violence. She may feel obliged to accept some responsibility for his violence and attempt to minimise its significance. Her acceptance of responsibility for her partner's behaviour may be accompanied by feelings of shame or guilt.

The therapist may help to establish a **context for safety and self-responsibility** by monitoring each partner's readiness to discuss openly sensitive issues, such as violence, throughout the initial couple contact. If the women begins to address her partner's violence, the therapist may interrupt and enquire of the man:

Can you handle Jill talking honestly about your violence?
Do you think it is safe for Jill to talk about your violence or would it be wiser for her to keep her mouth shut?

The therapist may enquire of the woman:
Do you think that Jack can handle you talking honestly about his violence or do you think he needs you to water it down a bit?
Do you think he can handle you speaking your true feelings or do you think he will crack up after the session?

The therapist can then check the man's opinion on these issues and enquire further:
Do you think that Jill will feel safe enough to talk openly here?
Do you think that Jill will be worried about what you will do when you both leave here?
Do you think that Jill can handle talking honestly about your violence or do you think that she is likely to feel disloyal, guilty or that she is letting you down?

The therapist can then seek the woman's opinion on these matters.

In this way, the therapist not only monitors each partner's perception of safety but can externalize fears and restraints to openness, invite challenge to these restraints and give permission for honest expression of feelings and opinions.

Both partners are invited to **externalize and challenge their own restraints to the man accepting responsibility for his violence.**

The woman is invited to examine her partner's pattern of reliance on her to take responsibility for his violence and to examine trends in this pattern over time:
How long has Jack been relying on you to:
- watch/look after his moods/feelings for him?
- put the brakes on his violence for him?
- forgive/put up with his violence?
- keep your thoughts/feelings to yourself?
- go along with his ideas?
- stay in the back seat of your relationship?
What signs are there that Jack is standing on his own two feet and becoming less reliant on you?
Is Jack relying on you more over time or is he becoming more able to stand on his own two feet?

Alan Jenkins

Is he becoming more reliant on you to take charge of his violence or is he setting his own limits more over time?
What do you think will happen if he continues to rely on you in this way? What would it mean for your relationship?
What would happen if you:
- stopped looking after his moods/feelings for him?
- no longer forgave/put up with violence?
- stopped keeping your thoughts and feelings to yourself?

The therapist may invite the woman to consider the **relative influence of socio-cultural and family traditions,** regarding "back seat-nurturance" roles for women, in her life. **Trends in time** may be examined by asking questions, like the following:

Do you think that Jill is taking more or less responsibility for your violence over time?
Do you think that Jill is:
- watching/looking after your feelings more or less over time?
- putting the brakes on, etc?
What tells you this?
Are you aware of times when Jill has refused to stay in the back seat of your relationship and stood up for what she believes?
Are you aware of times when Jill has practised being her own person and speaking her own mind, rather than pretending to be your person?
Do you think Jill is getting more into or more out of being a back seat nurturer over time?
Do you think that Jill is trying to carry more of your responsibilities in the relationship over time or is she leaving your responsibilities more to you to carry?
Do you think that Jill is feeling more entitled over time to - be her own person? - speak her own mind? - feel safe/treated respectfully? or is she feeling more guilty/disloyal about this over time?
Do you think that Jill would be prepared to stay in a relationship where she continued to be subject to violence and abuse?

I find it most helpful to first ask the man these questions and invite him to speculate and comment on his perceptions of his partner's experience and behaviour. I then ask the woman to comment and give her opinions. This kind of questioning process encourages greater sensitivity and invites couples to externalize restraints to self-responsibility in open discussion.

Irresistible invitations to self-responsibility can be delivered very effectively in a couple context. These invitations may be particularly compelling and challenging when one partner is asked to predict the other's responses. Strong invitations are provided for each partner to externalize and challenge their own restraining habits and ideas. For example, if the women states that she is not convinced that her partner could handle her speaking her own mind, then the onus is placed on the man to find ways with both words and actions to convince her.

The therapist may ask the woman:

Do you think that Jack could handle you speaking your mind or do you think that he needs you to protect him/look after his feelings, by pretending to go along with his ideas?

Do you think that Jack could handle it if you resigned from the back seat of your marriage?

Do you think he could handle you being your own person or do you think he needs you to pretend to be his person?

Do you think he wants to stand on his own two feet or do you think he would rather have you prop him up by looking after his feelings/moods for him?

Do you think that Jack needs you to stay in the back seat to have a marriage with you or could he handle you being in the front seat?

Do you think Jack wants to take charge of his own violence or do you think he needs you to do it for him?

Do you think Jack approves of you leaving the back seat/stopping taking responsibility for his violence?

What makes you think this?

What evidence have you seen that Jack wants it this way?

What evidence have you sen that Jack can handle you speaking your mind/disagreeing with him/making your own decisions, etc.?

The therapist can then check back with the man for his opinions on these matters before enquiring of him:

Do you think that Jill would feel safe enough to speak her mind at home or would she be too scared of a backlash from you?

What would you need to do to reassure her that she is safe no matter what she says or does?

What would you need to do to convince her that you are interested in her opinions?

Alan Jenkins

Do you think that Jill feels that it is safe for her to give up taking responsibility for your violence, by no longer walking on egg shells?

Do you think that Jill is ready to leave the back seat and join you in the front seat of the marriage?

Do you think that she is ready to give up looking after your feelings and start looking after her own more?

Do you think that she is ready to say "No" to things that she disagrees with or disapproves of?

Do you think she could handle putting her own needs forward after so much practise at trying to look after others needs?

Do you think Jill would feel right about being more of her own person or do you think she would feel too guilty in putting her own needs forward?

Do you think that Jill is ready to stand up to the feelings of guilt or selfishness that might accompany this change?

Do you think that Jill could stand up to her old habit of being sucked in and backing down, if your feelings got hurt?

What makes you think this?

What evidence have you seen that Jill is ready for this?

The therapist can then check back with the woman for her opinion on these matters. When the man argues that his partner **should** feel safe to speak her mind, etc., the woman can be invited to comment on her experience in recent situations:

When you last disagreed with Jack:

- what happened?

- how did he handle it?

- how did you handle it?

The onus is placed on the man to establish a safe environment and convince his partner that she is safe under all circumstances.

If the man is arguing for "standing on his own two feet" and is uncertain whether his partner could handle speaking her mind and "being her own person" due to feelings of guilt, disloyalty and misguided nurturance, the woman may be invited to put stronger arguments for self-responsibility.

If the woman feels safe enough and ready to practise taking less responsibility for her partner's feelings and behaviour and to practise "being her own person",then she may be invited to invent creative ways to **translate these ideas into actions**. Both partners may be invited to consider their readiness to take new action. I find it helpful to remind each of them of the fact that they have slavishly followed old habits for some time and that the pull of these old recipes for relating will prove almost irresistible at times. They are invited to **anticipate, predict and plan for obstacles** which they will encounter in their paths. It may be necessary to advise them to consider the wisdom of an initial period of **separation** or less frequent contact, in order to help establish independence and disrupt habitual, restraining patterns of interaction. Such advice can be shocking, at first, for couples who feel committed to staying together and they may argue strongly against the idea. The therapist should not back down but remind them of the difficulty of changing old habits whilst spending so much time together and inform them that couples who separate for a time are generally more successful in changing these habits. If the couple insist on maintaining the amount of contact with each other, they can be invited to test their abilities to stand up to unhelpful habits, under such challenging circumstances, over a period of time and to reconsider the need for a period of separation at the next appointment. In this way, whatever the couple decides, interactional restraints to self-responsibility can be more potently externalized and challenged.

The therapist may help the woman to develop **realistic criteria for evaluating change** in her partner's behaviour. She is encouraged to monitor objective evidence of respectful behaviour as opposed to promises and statements of intent. In this way, she is encouraged to use behavioural evidence rather than feelings of obligation, hope and wishful thinking, in order to make judgements about trends in violence and abuse in the relationship.

The woman is advised to **avoid premature trust** in her partner's changes, with respect to violence. She is encouraged to continue to monitor the evidence provided by her partner's actions and to avoid letting go of fear, doubt and mistrust until she is convinced, beyond a shadow of doubt, that the changes have withstood the test of time and of challenging circumstances. Permission for the woman to be cautious and take her time in accepting her partners changes, helps challenge traditions of female obligation which suggest that she should have faith in his stated intentions and the continuation of new behaviours, regardless of past evidence to the contrary.

The man is continually reminded that the onus is on him to demonstrate long term change before expecting his partner to trust him or fully commit herself to the relationship. He may be encouraged to monitor nd take responsibility for his own self-righteous feelings and thoughts which are experienced when his partner does not immediately embrace his changes. It may be helpful to advise him to be vigilant for any signs of his partner establishing closeness or trusting his changes prematurely, perhaps out of a sense of obligation or responsibility.

The man is also invited to extend his **understanding and sensitivity, particularly towards his partner's experience**. The woman may be asked, in his presence:

Do you think Jack understands what he has put you through - why you have been so fearful - why you have so little trust in him?

Do you think he understands how long it may take to develop trust in him again - that you may never trust him fully again?

Do you think that he can respect your feelings or do you think he will succumb to impatience/insensitivity and try to demand that you trust him prematurely?

Do you think that he is prepared to wait however long it takes to earn your trust and respect - in your time, or do you think he will try to demand it back - in his time?

The therapist can then check with the man for his opinions on these matters. Once again, the onus is on him to develop and act on this understanding and sensitivity.

When there is evidence that the man is taking responsibility for his own feelings and has not engaged in violence for some time, the therapist may encourage **conflict testing**. The man is invited to test himself fully by facing up to arguments and challenging situations in order to consolidate his ability to behave non-violently under challenging circumstances. This strategy can help him to develop confidence in his own ability to think clearly, avoid surrendering to insecure feelings and stay in charge of his actions, regardless of the circumstances in which he finds himself. He is advised against developing a false sense of confidence and relying on strategies which involve avoiding arguments or falling back into the pattern of expecting his partner to back off and keep the peace. The notion is put forward that he must be able to handle high levels of behaviour which he may regard as unreasonable or provocative, without resorting to violence, before he can regard himself as having quit violence. *Nick had just finished a men's group and was feeling confident because he had not behaved in a violent way towards his wife, Julie, in four months.*

When Nick and Julie were interviewed together, Nick proudly exclaimed that they had not even had an argument in this time. It soon became apparent that Julie had been "keeping my mouth shut" and avoiding conflict by deferring to Nick in areas of potential disagreement, for fear that "Nick might return to the way he was".

Nick was asked whether he could genuinely feel confident in his ability to leave violence behind him unless he faced arguments with Julie without resorting to violent behaviour. He was asked whether he needed Julie's protection or whether he could handle her saying what she really thinks. In this way, the therapist was able to "prescribe arguments" and challenge both Nick and Julie to take further steps towards establishing and maintaining a non-violent relationship.

Both partners are encouraged to develop a healthy attitude towards arguments and to understand the important role that arguments play in the normal development of relationships. Once the woman no longer feels restrained by obligation and fear, it is inevitable that she will feel safer in expressing her feelings and differences. The man is encouraged to prepare himself for the inevitable increase in arguments and disagreements and to regard this as a healthy sign of change as well as an opportunity for practise in non-violent conflict.

Both partners may be invited to strive for **balance** in terms of who takes **responsibility for maintenance of the relationship**. This is especially important in relationships where the woman has worked hardest for the social and emotional responsibilities. She may experience her partner as "selfish", "lazy" or "uncaring". He is likely to experience her as "nagging" and "never satisfied".

The woman may be asked questions like the following:

Do you think Jack wants to make a contribution to your marriage or do you think he is prepared to leave it up to you to take responsibility for the marriage?

Do you think Jack wants to take an equal share of responsibility in your marriage or do you think he wants you to carry some of his load for him?

Do you think that Jack could handle this after having relied on you for so long?

Do you think Jack could handle it if you stop reminding him and getting on his back or do you think he needs you to be on his back?"

The therapist can check back with the man for his opinions on these matters before asking him:

Do you think that Jill is ready and prepared to share responsibility in the marriage?

Do you think that she could handle stepping back - not reminding you etc., after so much practise?

Do you think she could handle you making your own contributions in your own ways or do you think that she needs you do it her way?

Both partners are encouraged to continue to discover ways to maintain a healthy **balance between separateness/independence and togetherness** in their relationship. This may mean developing more separate interests and activities; a process which usually begins in the initial period of separation, when both partners begin to develop a sense of independence. Initial gains, however, may be lost when the couple reunites, unless there is an emphasis placed on the importance of separateness. Both partners are encouraged to find active ways to show respect for each others separateness and independence and to challenge cultural myths regarding togetherness in relationships.

Couple therapy does not always lead to maintenance of the relationship. The goals are mutual respect, sensitivity and cessation of abuse. One or both partners may decide to terminate the relationship.

When one or both partners decide to separate, difficulties are often experienced in successfully achieving the separation. These difficulties can be seen to result from the highly mutually dependent nature of the relationship. Sometimes the separation is only partially achieved. Both partners may live in separate houses but still maintain considerable "investment" with each other in the same manner as before - that is one which is based on notions of male ownership and female obligation. Such partial separations may endure for long periods of time with both partners reporting considerable dissatisfaction and distress. Sometimes the couple may cohabit once again and re-establish the original pattern of violence. e.g. One couple described their "drift" back together, *because we were both lonely and unhappy and there was nothing else to do.*

Some men still attempt to exert ownership over their ex-partners following separation, particularly if the ex-partners have initiated the separation. They may engage in attempts to follow ex-partners around in obvious ways, make frequent phone calls, question their ex-partner's friends regarding their actions and whereabouts, drive past their ex-partner's house and engage in other forms of pursuit for long periods of time, especially if the ex-partners do not take strong action to stop this.

These men often state that they have finished with the relationship but act in ways that indicate that they are still highly invested. This contradiction can be pointed out and the consequences of maintaining the investment can be predicted. For example:
Greg was attending a men's group. He had been separated from his wife Chris for three months, at her instigation. She was showing no signs of wanting to re-establish the relationship and was living at an address unknown to Greg. Greg told the group that his relationship with Chris was finished - "I don't give a stuff about her anymore" and that he was now "looking after

Alan Jenkins

myself and my own life". He then related how he had called Chris a "fucking slut" after meeting her and discovering that she had gone out with another man. He also cut up his marriage certificate and mailed it to her parents along with his wedding ring and then reported to the Department of Social Security that she was illegally claiming a benefit. Later, he spent considerable time and energy finding out her address and sent her a letter, telling her that he didn't care a bit about her anymore. Greg reported that he had met with Chris on another occasion and given her some "helpful advice and support" regarding difficulties that she was having with her parents.

The contradiction between Greg's stated intention - to live his own life - and his actions was pointed out to him as were some of the different ways in which he was attempting to maintain his investment with Chris. The tendency to maintain a relationship based on vengeance along with the tendency to try to establish a relationship as Chris' "social worker" and try to solve her problems, were discussed. Predictions were made about the consequences of Greg continuing this investment. One group member suggested that Greg's motto was "Don't get mad, get even". Greg responded to these suggestions with increased resolve to avoid making contact with Chris, either directly or indirectly and to practise living his own life.

Some women also continue to invest in the relationship after separation. This investment may be unwanted and based on fear, or unwitting and based on notions of female obligation. Such a woman may tolerate her ex-partner's intrusive ownership displays and protect him from legal consequences. She may hope that his pursuit behaviour will stop without her needing to take firm action. She may feel obligated to try to help her ex-partner to deal with his problems by offering emotional support or "a shoulder to cry on." One woman explained that if she had sex with her ex-partner on one occasion when he was feeling distressed and "needing it", then he might go away and leave her alone in the future. Of course, consideration for the woman's safety must be taken if she decides to stop investing in a relationship.

Once again the consequences of these actions for both persons, in terms of successfully establishing separate and fulfilling lifestyles can be predicted and discussed. If either partner continues to invest energy in a past relationship, then they will be unlikely to be able to face the challenge of developing a new life style and may return to unsatisfactory relationships out of a sense of desperation and loneliness.

PART III

THE PROCESS OF ENGAGEMENT OF MEN WHO SEXUALLY ABUSE CHILDREN

*When I think about how I was "Vicky's" dad and I just
set her up and used her for my own sexual feelings - I
treated her like she was nothing at all - not my daughter.
I knew it was wrong but I didn't care. I didn't even think
of "Vicky's" feelings at all - I even tried to make is
sound O.K. - like it really was O.K. for her. When she
told (partner) I called her a liar and told her not to
make up stories.*

*I've destroyed something inside her - what I've done
won't ever go away. She'll carry what I've done to her
for ever.*

*Statement by an abusive man
in therapy, 1989*

Alan Jenkins

There has been considerable debate as to whether child sexual offenders should be offered therapy or punished through the criminal justice system (Cashmore & Horsky 1987; Glaser 1988). I do not regard these options as alternatives and believe that therapeutic programmes should operate within the context of the criminal justice system. To decriminalize or remove sanctions for sexual assault would do little to promote responsible behaviour and a safe environment in the wider community. Such a step would be unlikely to reduce sexually irresponsible behaviour or encourage many offenders to seek therapy. The community is entitled to **expect** offenders to seek therapy and change their behaviour and to **expect** the criminal justice system to act to ensure that this happens and intervene strongly it if does not. Sexual offenders commence therapy as a result of a variety of largely external motivations (e.g. fear of imprisonment or loss of family support). It is the therapist's role to help these men discover more appropriate reasons for continuing therapy which centre around personal responsibility for abusive behaviour. The criminal justice system has an important role in ensuring initial co-operation in therapy until new internal motivations are evident. Monitoring of goal attainment in therapy should also be a role of the criminal justice system, in order to minimise risk to the community. A number of options for locating therapy within the criminal justice system have been developed including pre-trial diversionary systems and various forms of sentencing options for offenders (Bulkey & Davidson 1981; South Australian Government Task Force on Child Sexual Abuse 1986; Giaretto 1981).

Attempts to control and prevent sexual assault based on punishment and deterrent models alone, appear to be spectacularly unsuccessful (Knopp 1984). Child sexual offences are extremely prevalent in our society and it appears that less than 10% of sexual assaults are reported to police and less than one percent result in arrest, conviction and imprisonment of the offender (Russell 1984). When a child sexual offence is notified, generally little is done to address the offender's behaviour. Police are unlikely to take action in the majority of cases, particularly when very young children are involved, due to the difficulty in obtaining evidence which would be regarded as valid and reliable in a courtroom. It is evident that a strong yet inadvertent incentive exists, in the criminal justice system, for men to behave irresponsibly following notification. Men who acknowledge their offences are likely to be charged and imprisoned. Men who deny their offences are likely to be left alone and face no consequences. In other words, it "pays" to be irresponsible. Not surprisingly, many offenders re-offend, either in the same or in a different setting.

The small percentage of offenders who are imprisoned generally receive little help to change their offending behaviour. Punishment and imprisonment do nothing to alter the factors which have restrained the man from engaging in responsible behaviour. Most prison settings inadvertently promote further irresponsible behaviour. There is little opportunity for the learning and practice of responsible behaviour within such a highly structured and supervised prison regime. Many sexual offenders are physically and emotionally abused by other prisoners, sometimes even prison authorities. Facilities for protective isolation of sexual offenders, designed to prevent prisoner abuse, can promote subcultures in which abusive behaviour is condoned and promoted. Consequently, there is little opportunity for prisoners to face responsibility and develop self-reliance and self-esteem. When released, many feel bitter and persecuted and appear to have lost integrity and self-reliance. In this state, they are prone to sink further into a cycle of irresponsible behaviour (Knopp, 1984).

I believe that abusive men have a responsibility to face up to and accept full responsibility for their abuse. This needs to happen in a "public" way so that those who have been harmed by the abuse can be helped to throw off some of the burden of secrecy and responsibility what has been dumped on them. A declaration of acceptance of responsibility to all family members and those influenced by the abuse, helps to counteract the secrecy, fear and protective loyalty which serve to maintain abuse-related trauma. The offender is less likely to hide behind a veil of secrecy and more able to face and deal with his abusive behaviour. This process is especially relevant in situations in which abusive men stay with, rejoin or maintain contact with families in which they have abused.

Alan Jenkins

Therapists who work with sexual offenders have a responsibility, not just to their client's needs, but to ensure that therapeutic programmes are sensitive to the needs and feelings of family members and others influenced by the abuse as well as to the wider community. In this context, issues of confidentiality, as applied to other areas of counselling, need to be reassessed. I subscribe to the notion of "limited confidentiality" which is discussed on page 123, Part III.

As with spouse abusers, sexual offenders are generally regarded as poorly motivated and resistant to therapeutic approaches (Knopp, 1984; McFarlane & Buckley, 1982). The sexual offender, like the spouse abuser, may feel considerable distress and even despair regarding his abusive behaviour, regardless of motivation to seek therapy. Most offenders are aware that their behaviour is illegal and morally wrong but have little awareness of the impact it has upon others. Many child sexual offenders would like to cease their abusive behaviour. Like spouse abusers, however, they are well practised at avoiding responsibility for their own actions and attributing it to external events or other people. They remain highly restrained and fail to take effective action to cease the abuse. Other people tend to be "invited" or coerced into attending to and taking responsibility for the abusive behaviour by virtue of the man's failure to do so. Consequently, the man will have developed well established habits of reliance upon others to worry about, try to prevent and avoid the abuse, maintain secrecy and set limits on his behaviour. He becomes rapidly caught up in an escalating cycle of irresponsibility and reliance on others to take responsibility for him.

The man seldom attends therapy on his own initiative. Therapy is usually precipitated by disclosure of the victim, threats of welfare or police action or family sanctions. Not surprisingly, he is likely to display irresponsible behaviour to the therapist, who may find the man's "invitations" to take responsibility for him quire irresistible, especially given that the victim is a child.

The therapist is faced with identical issues to those in working with spouse abusers. However, sexual offenders are likely to display even more irresponsible behaviour and offer more compelling "invitations" to the therapist to take responsibility. This tends to be the case because child sexual offences carry a greater threat of police, legal and welfare intervention, a greater threat of marital and family dissolution and greater societal disapproval and condemnation than offences of spouse abuse.

Child sexual offenders struggle to deal with deep and pervasive feelings of shame about their actions and they panic about consequences to themselves. In my experience, child sexual offenders are often more highly restrained and show higher levels of avoidance of responsibility and reliance on others than spouse abusers who present for therapy.

The principles of therapeutic engagement presented for work with male spouse abusers (see page 60) may be applied to both adult and adolescent sexual offenders. The following seven steps constitute a specific model for engagement of men referred following sexual offences against children who are closely related, generally by kinship ties:

---------- Invite the man to attend to the abuse;

---------- Invite the man to establish a mission in responsibility;

---------- Invite the man to consider his readiness to embark on a mission in responsibility;

---------- Implementing the mission - Part I, Facing the Abuse;

---------- Implementing the mission - Part II, Contextualising the abuse;

---------- Implementing the mission - Part III, Demonstrating responsibility;

---------- Implementing the mission - Part IV, Preventing relapse.

Many of the ideas presented may be used with other sexual offences, and these applications should be considered in the light of recent findings which indicate a wide variety and frequency of "undetected" sexual offences for some offenders (Abel et al 1988). Once again the aim of the model is to facilitate these men to take responsibility for their abusive behaviour, although its application with child sexual offenders involves some different emphases from the process with spouse abusers.

Alan Jenkins

INVITE THE MAN TO ATTEND TO THE ABUSE

Before meeting with the man and asking his reasons for attendance, I attempt to get as much information as I can about alleged incidents of abuse, from the referral source. This includes details of allegations, assessments of the victim, opinions of family members and police statements. I find it helpful to consider the man's account of events in the context of others' beliefs and reactions.

If the abuse is alleged to be recent, and if the victim is a family member, the man may be facing police charges and may have been advised by welfare authorities to leave the family home.

He may present protesting his innocence and claim that he has been set up or misunderstood. An inventory of mistakes and oversights by the welfare authorities may be presented or he may be preoccupied with inconsistencies and errors in the victim's account of events. In this way, the therapist is invited to judge the man's guilt or innocence and attend to details which "prove" that he has been wrongly accused and hard done by.

Alternatively, the man will partially acknowledge or very rarely, fully acknowledge his offences. The extent of acknowledgement may be slight at this stage.

e.g. I was just holding her and perhaps my hand slipped and it might have touched her down there.

This acknowledgement is usually accompanied by explanations and justifications which reflect avoidance or denial of responsibility. These explanations and justifications may be considered in terms of levels of denial of responsibility as shown in Figure 1.

Figure 1

Levels of Denial of Responsibility

1. **Denial of the Existence or Extent of Abuse**

   "She misinterpreted my actions"

   "I was only playing with her/dressing her/applying ointment"

   "I might have accidentally touched her"

   "She must have mistaken me for someone else"

   "Her mother/welfare workers have set her up to say this"

   "I can't remember"

2. **Denial of the Significance of Abuse**

   "I didn't hurt her" "She enjoyed it too"

   "I only touched her...I didn't have sex with her"

   "It's been blown out of all proportion"

   "I was only showing caring"

   "Perhaps I loved her too much"

   "It wasn't a sexual thing - I didn't feel any sexual pleasure"

   "It hasn't affected her in any way - she runs up to see me/tells me she loves me/doesn't avoid me"

   "I was teaching her about sex"

   "I wanted her first time to be good"

3. **Denial of Responsibility for the Abuse**

   "She wanted me to do it/started it/asked for it"

   "I would have stopped if she had said she didn't want me to do it"

   "I was drunk.....asleep"

   "I was under stress/had marriage problems"

   "It just happened - I don't know how or why"

4. **Denial of the Likelihood of re-occurrence of Abuse**

   "It won't happen again"

   "I'd never put myself through all this again"

   "I no longer have any sexual urges towards the (victim)"

   "I'm putting all my energy into work now"

   "I have found the Lord"

   "I've paid my debt to society"

   "It's all behind me now - I want to look to the future"

   "I just want all of us to get on with our lives now"

Alan Jenkins

The man may present desperate invitations for the therapist to ignore or discount abusive incidents and his responsibility for them. He may attempt to convince the therapist that his wife or children need him home and to support him reuniting with his family.

Alternatively, the man may present in a "helpless" state and directly invite the therapist to take responsibility for him by helping him to understand why he has offended, castigating him, hearing his "confession" or telling him what to do.

As with the spouse abuser, I find it helpful to decline these invitations to ignore the abuse and to attribute responsibility externally and instead invite the man to describe events which have led to him attending his appointment at this time. After briefly listening to his explanations, I interrupt and invite him to attend to details of actual events which have taken place:

How did the abuse/allegations come out into the open?
When did you first hear about this disclosure?
How were you told?
What did you do and say?
What did others do and say?
What have you done/others done since then?
Who have you talked to about the abuse/allegations?
How did they react/what did they do/say?
What contact have you had with welfare authorities/police?

Other strategies for helping the man to attend to factual events are detailed in the section on spouse abuse (see "Invite the Man to Address his Violence" - page 64). The therapist can then invite the man to attend to the impact of these events on his own and others' lives:

How have these incidents/allegations affected you?
Where has this left you?
How have these events/allegations affected Jill/(the victim)/other family members?
What do you think Jill thought/felt when she first confronted you?
What do you think Jill thinks/feels now?
What do you think (the victim) thinks/feels now?
What do you think Jill thinks should happen now?
What do you think (the victim) thinks should happen now?
"What do you think the welfare authorities think should happen now?

In this way the man is invited to speculate about others' experiences, feelings and wishes, as they occurred, rather than remain preoccupied with his own irresponsible ideas. A process for asking these questions is detailed in the section on spouse abuse (see "Invite the Man to Address his Violence" - page 64).

The therapist remains vigilant for any evidence of the man accepting responsibility for his abuse and is ready to acknowledge and express respect for his strength and courage in taking such steps. If he acknowledges any truth to the allegations, the therapist may respond in ways similar to those detailed in the corresponding section on spouse abuse (see page 66). I label abusive behaviour clearly as "abuse", from the commencement of therapy. I avoid using terms such as "fondling" and "interfering" which can serve to detract from the seriousness of the abuse and the extent of the man's facing up:

It takes a lot of courage to face up to the fact that you sexually abused your stepdaughter. Most men can't face it and cop out pretending that nothing happened. They run from their fears and shame and never find the courage to make a stand to try to put things right.

When did you first decide to face up to it?

What made you decide to face up to it?

What did you do when you were first confronted with the allegations?

How did you manage to face the truth?

It would have been a lot easier to cop out.

Who have you faced up to and told the truth to?

What does this say about you as a person/as a parent?

If the man acknowledges other responsible steps such as moving out of the family home, if the victim is a family member, or finding ways to respect the victim's needs for space and privacy, these steps can also be labelled and highlighted as courageous and responsible. The therapist may inquire as to how the man decided and managed to take such steps in the light of his previously disrespectful and irresponsible behaviour.

I find it useful to explain, early in the first interview, the notion of "limited confidentiality". I am obliged to notify any evidence of child abuse which has not already been reported. Other information is confidential within certain limits. It is stressed that any work with the man must be sensitive to the needs and feelings of those affected by his abuse and the general community's right to safety. No therapeutic work will knowingly be commenced which might disadvantage or further victimize others. Consequently, it is desirable for the therapist to have some ongoing contact with other family members and therapists involved. I ask the man's permission to make contact with other family members or persons influenced by the abuse in order to understand their wishes and needs. If this permission was declined, I would feel obliged to terminate therapy.

If family reunion or access with the victim is desired, it will be necessary for the therapist to discuss the man's progress in therapy with family members, therapists and welfare workers and perhaps involve them in therapy sessions. If court reports are requested, the therapist will need to document the same information for the criminal justice system. I agree to discuss these matters first with the man but maintain the right to inform others of relevant information in either of the above circumstances.

TOTAL DENIAL

Many men completely deny that there is any truth whatsoever to the child's allegations. Of course, these men are unlikely to present in counselling settings. However, I occasionally see men who present with total denial, often in the face of convincing evidence that the alleged abuse has in fact taken place.

I generally find it unhelpful to openly confront and challenge these men, even when the evidence of their abuse seems convincing. The risk of "inviting" the man to behave more irresponsibly in therapy is great under these circumstances. This is particularly the case if the man has made no acknowledgement to any other person, has told his story many times and has received comforting legal advice. Direct confrontation is also unhelpful when other family members, such as the man's partner, are disbelieving of the allegations and supporting the man in his denial. Direct confrontation is likely to result in escalating the tendency for family members to dismiss the allegations and form a tighter alliance against "intrusive" external authorities who are seen as wanting to destroy the family. Even victims of abuse who have disclosed, can be drawn into this alliance in which abuse is "forgotten" in the struggle to preserve the family and protect family members. These alliances lead to a greater risk of further abuse.

When the family members, especially partners, are ambivalent and uncertain about who to believe, it is often more helpful to talk with them and help them to find ways to evaluate events which have taken place and the meaning of these events. Confrontation of the man by family members will generally be more helpful than confrontation by professionals or welfare authorities. The therapist, of course, must also be open to the possibility that there is no truth to the allegations.

When working with men who totally deny, I find it helpful to be patient and to decline the man's invitations for me to make judgements or try to determine the truth of the matter. I try to keep my options open and not to foreclose on believing any particular version of events. Above all, I try to avoid giving the man practice in expressing denial and avoidance of responsibility. If there is truth to the allegations I do not want to "invite" him to paint himself further into a corner of denial and pretence. In many cases, I appear to achieve little more than successfully declining the man's invitations. This is better, however, than contributing towards an escalation if an irresponsible story.

Men who present with total denial tend to have offences or alleged offences against close relatives or family members. They present in a state of panic and desperation, facing possible police charges or having been advised to move out of the family home by welfare authorities. Alternatively, they are referred by a parole officer after having served a prison sentence and are subject to parole and welfare restrictions on resuming contact with their families.

As previously mentioned, I listen briefly to the man's story before inviting him to detail events which have led up to his attendance, what these events have meant to him and to others, what he thinks should happen now and what he thinks others think should happen now. It can be helpful to highlight any differences between his perceptions in these matters and his beliefs about others' perceptions.

In particular, I attempt to highlight and acknowledge what the man's goals are and what is important to him now. Generally these men are feeling terrified and desperate at the threat of losing their families and of possible legal sanctions. I find it helpful to acknowledge my understanding of the importance of the man's family to him, the pain and desperation he is feeling at being separate from them and his fear of losing them along with any worries he expresses about their welfare.

When I believe that the man has heard me express some of his feelings and concerns, I ask his permission for me to take time to explain the nature of my role and the differences between the goals of my clinic and those of welfare or correctional agencies. I explain that the role of welfare authorities is child protection and continue:

Here, we work with men and sometimes members of their families, after abuse has occurred or been alleged. We are concerned with every member of the family and try to find ways that will help resolve problems around the abuse that will help all family members and be sensitive to each person's needs and feelings. When all members of a family want to reunite, we try to help with this and look at how it can happen in a way which will benefit all members of a family. This is one our main roles.

Having established a sphere of interest which extends wider than the man's needs and feelings, I then ask his permission to give him further information which relates to my stand about truth and allegations:

Can I give you some information that we give to all men who come here in your circumstances.

We are not lawyers or police and we cannot determine the truth of the matter. Only you and (the victim) know this. We cannot hope to make judgements about the truth. Consequently, we find it most helpful to keep our options open, if we are to be of any help to you and others in your family. It doesn't help anyone if we pretend we can get to the truth of the matter ourselves. Only you and the victim will ever know this.

I talk in the third person and present some general information about men who present with total denial. If the man interrupts me or attempts to protest his innocence, I patiently reiterate my inability to judge his innocence or guilt and explain again the need to inform all men who attend this clinic of the way that we work and think about these situations. I then ask:

Can you handle my continuing?

In 99% of the cases we see, where things are unclear, there turns out to be at least a grain of truth in the allegations. We also know that when there is some truth to allegations, most men find it extremely difficult to come here. When there is some truth to allegations, most men are not able to face this at first - particularly when they first come here. We understand this and in fact don't expect that kind of facing up at first.

I then detail some of the reasons as why it is difficult for men to face up to abuse and in this way try to externalize some restraints to facing up:

Most men I have met find it almost impossible to face up to what they have done to their daughter. Most I have met feel an overwhelming sense of shame when they think about it. They can't understand why it had happened and feel that it is totally out of character for them to have behaved in such a way. Consequently, most men push it right to the back of their minds. Many have wound up painting themselves into a corner where it becomes harder and harder to face up to it. They would like to face it but now it seems too big a step to back down and face the consequences they fear. Some men have pushed it so far to the back of their minds that they have almost forgotten what happened and need time to look back and recall it.

In order to further clarify and externalize restraints to facing up to the abuse, I then explain some of the things that I have discovered about men who have sexually abused:

There are several things that I have learned with men when there is some truth to allegations. Firstly, I have met very few men who have wanted to hurt or maltreat their children. The men I have worked with have generally been very caring persons and not the monsters that tend to get talked about in newspapers. Most men I have worked with have wanted to have loving and caring relationships and somehow sex has got in the way of this and the whole thing feels like it has got out of control. They have not wanted to hurt the people they love.

Secondly, most men I have worked with have wanted to stop the abuse but have not known how. Many have wanted help but have not known how to ask. Many have realised that they have a problem that they need to address but don't know how. They feel that they have been going around and around in circles.

Thirdly, most men feel absolute panic when it comes out into the open. They are still reeling from the shock waves when they first come here. They fear they will lose their family, their job, their freedom and perhaps their self-respect completely. This of course, is the thing that makes it so difficult to face the problem.

or

Thirdly, men who have served time generally only wind up feeling angry, resentful and lost when they come out of prison. Most know they needed some help but also know they didn't get it; only punishment. Many have only lost more self-respect and don't how to begin to get it back.

Fourthly, most men I meet want to do whatever they can to make up for having let their kids and their family down. They want to help try to put things right for others they have hurt - they don't want them to suffer.

Alan Jenkins

I usually explain to all men that come here that I can understand why it is not possible to face up to it at first when there is some truth to allegations.

I then invite the man to receive some more information which serves to highlight a dilemma which he may well already have experienced but tries not to think about. This dilemma contains an invitation to attend to and face up to abusive behaviour as well as an expression of the therapist's willingness to respect and support the man in any steps he takes to face up. The dilemma provides an invitation to weigh up the consequences and meanings of facing versus denying abusive behaviour.

When there is some truth to allegations and the man wants to help the victim and try to build a new and more caring family life, then I think it is important that he weighs up the options himself and makes his own decisions. I think that is his job and it isn't up to others to push him in any direction. A man should decide for himself whether to face up to or cop out and run away from his responsibilities.

When I meet the man he is usually reeling from the shockwaves of having it come out into the open and panicking that things will get worse if he faces up to it (or feeling fed up and up to his neck in resentment after serving time and just wanting to forget the whole thing and be left alone).

I usually explain that I can understand that the man is reeling from the shock of it coming out in the open (wanting to forget the whole thing) but he is talking about his family and his future - big decisions - and it is wise to weigh it up carefully.

If he faces up, it provides the only way that a rift in the family can be possibly healed - the only way respect and trust can be regained - the only way that a family can get together in way that is real and not pretending - the only way to real closeness and genuine forgiveness. Copping out and running away is the best recipe for living a lie and for having a family life based on disrespect and fear. I usually ask men to consider:
Would it be possible to have a family life based on respect and trust without the guy facing up to what he has done?

Facing up provides the only way that the guy can help the child to reclaim his/her life and minimise the scarring and damage that abuse so often causes - the only way the guy can possibly begin to help and try to put things right and make amends for what he has done. I usually ask men to consider:

Would you be prepared to let the child carry around your load of responsibility instead of carrying it on your own shoulders?

Would you be prepared to let the child do your suffering for you?

Would you be prepared to sacrifice the child's life so you can avoid the consequences of your actions?

Would you be prepared to let the child carry the can for you for the rest of his/her life or could handle standing on your own two feet and carry your own load yourself so that the child is free to heal him/herself and put the abuse behind him/her?

Facing up provides the only way that the welfare/courts can see that the man is genuinely taking some responsibility for what he did. It provides the only way that the welfare system can justify pulling out of your life and that the court is able to see the other side of you and take this into consideration in deciding what the consequences will be. Facing up provides one of the only real justifications for a sentence being suspended or reduced - if a judge can see that you are serious in wanting to do something about your problem. I usually ask men to consider:

Would you be prepared to go through with calling the child a liar and subjecting him/her to further abuse of going through the courts to try to avoid the possible consequences?

I ask men to consider:

What this would mean for your future, your relationship with the child and your own self-respect?

Facing up offers the only way that a man can develop some self-respect and learn to live with himself instead of living a lie and being constantly on the run from himself. I usually ask men to consider:

Could you actually face yourself if you left it for the child and others in the family to carry the can for you?

When highlighting this dilemma, I attend to the man's non-verbal responses as he listens. The man will often inadvertently nod or shake his head or give other cues which can alert the therapist to issues which are salient for the man and can be reiterated. I occasionally "lapse" from the third person to the first person when talking about issues which appear to be salient ones, in order to invite the man to consider taking a step closer towards committing himself to facing his abuse.

It is helpful to express my willingness to provide support for the man in facing up if there is "a grain of truth" to the allegations.

Alan Jenkins

I usually explain to men that I will back them up to the hilt if they are able to face up to abuse they have carried out. I explain that I am willing to help them to put things on the right track and support them in their dealings with the welfare and the parole/court systems. I explain that I have a lot of respect for men who can handle this responsibility and that there are ways they can start to put things right and not only help themselves but help others in the family to overcome the damage that has been done.

This may sound weird, but I usually explain to men that I hope that there is at least a grain of truth to allegations. In this case that it means it is possible to begin to put things right and to see whether your goals can be achieved. It means that the situation can be made clear to everyone and there is a chance for everyone to respect each other again and build new and happier lives.

I usually terminate the interview with an invitation for the man to take this information away and give it consideration:

I think it is important that you give this information consideration before we meet again and talk further. I think it is vital that you weigh it up and make your own decision. As I explained, I believe it is important for me to keep my options open because I know that for many men that I have worked with, they need plenty of time to make the wisest decision for themselves and for their families.

I imagine that your family is extremely important to you?

I imagine that the child and his/her future are pretty important to you?

I imagine that you want a family life that is based on trust and respect rather than on fear and pretending?

I generally ask the man's permission to make contact with other family members and relevant persons in order to understand their feelings and wishes at this time and arrange a new appointment time. The man will probably leave the appointment feeling considerable discomfort. If there is truth to the allegations, he is likely to experience considerable dissonance as he weighs up this dilemma. My aim is to structure any further interviews in ways which will make it difficult for him to avoid this dissonance, by declining to discuss other matters and continuing to invite the man to attend to the same dilemma. The man may become angry with the therapist who uses this strategy. I find it helpful, however, to calmly and firmly explain again the need to keep my options open and allow plenty of time, given my experience in working in these situations. Also, I find it helpful to explain this dilemma to the man's partner or other relevant persons who may be influential in his life. Other persons will then be less likely to attend to the man's protestations of innocence and help him to face his dilemma. Men who protest their innocence in the face of strong evidence to the contrary, must at least face the fact that the victim believes that s/he has been abused by the man. This means, at the least, that the victim is not convinced that the man can and does respect appropriate boundaries and differences between an adult and a child. In other words, the man has failed to help the child understand that he respects appropriate adult - child boundaries and that he would never violate them. At the least, the man must take responsibility to own that he has failed to convince the victim that s/he is safe with him and will be appropriately protected and respected by him.

INVITE THE MAN TO ESTABLISH A MISSION IN RESPONSIBILITY.

When there is some acknowledgement of the abuse, even if only partial and still accompanied by considerable denial of responsibility, (e.g. *I might have touched her once - it was only a game - it wasn't really a sexual thing*),the therapist may invite the man to establish a mission in responsibility. The mission is based on an invitation for the man to do more than argue for a non-abusive lifestyle but to argue also for facing up to and accepting responsibility for his past abusive behaviour.

The man is invited to consider three broad goals for his mission:
---------- assisting those he has victimized,
---------- preventing further abuse,
---------- developing self-respect and integrity.

The mission is a medium for helping the man to discover his **own** integrity and his **own** capacity to face responsibility. As with the spouse abuser, it is assumed that the man wants respectful relationships with others, particularly family members, and does not want to continue his abusive behaviour. However, he is behaving and thinking in a manner consistent with his restrained beliefs, which has prevented him from accepting responsibility for his behaviour and from discovering more effective and respectful ways of relating (see "Invite the Man to Argue for a Non-Violent Relationship - page 68).

As with the spouse abuser, the man's mission is derived from his own expressed goals and desires (see page 69). When discussing the man's account of events which have led up to the appointment and the meaning he has attributed to these events, the therapist will rapidly become aware of the man's concerns and agenda for therapy.

These will generally relate to:-
---------- panic at the threat of imprisonment and the thought of losing everything and a desperate desire to avoid these possibilities.
---------- extreme fears of losing his family. This may be expressed in terms of a desperate desire for forgiveness and forgetting - to

return to "normal family life" as quickly as possible. He may express concern for the welfare of other family members, perhaps believing that they are being traumatized by his absence and unable to cope without him. This fear and concern may be associated with a self-righteous preoccupation with the "unfairness" of welfare or parole authorities who are regarded as the obstacles preventing reunion with his family.

---------- fears and concerns about the meaning of his abusive behaviour, the likelihood of its recurrence and associated feelings of shame, self-doubt and self-disgust. These may be expressed as intellectual preoccupation with the question, "Why did I do it?" Quite commonly these fears and concerns are avoided and pushed out of awareness wherever possible. This avoidance may be based on the premise, "If I don't look at it and think of other things, it will go away." More rarely, the man expresses concerns that he may re-offend in the future.

It is helpful for the therapist to acknowledge the man's fears and concerns and to let him know that they have been heard and understood. At the same time the therapist should decline invitations to confirm restrained ideas associated with them as well as implicit "invitations" to correct them. Instead, the therapist may attend to the man's goals in a way that invites him to consider and argue for the kind of relationships he really desires.

INVITATIONS TO ASSIST THOSE VICTIMIZED BY THE ABUSE

I shall describe these invitations in relation to a common form of presentation in which a man who has abused a family member is living separately from his family, as a result of welfare or parole restrictions but is preoccupied with reuniting with his family. Such men are extremely reliant on the support of family members and desperate to "get back to a normal family life" and help family members who are seen as needing the man's help and support.

The therapist may attend to the man's desire to reunite with his family without endorsing this as a step which should take place now or even in the future:

I now understand that your family is very important to you. I imagine that it is extremely worrying/frightening/distressing for you to be apart from them

*and not know what is happening. I understand that you are not only worried
about what will happen to you but also what will happen to them.*
How are you handling this?
alternatively the therapist may say:
*I imagine it has been terribly difficult coping without them for two years while
you were on the inside - not being able to be with them, share in their lives
and help them.*
How have you handled this?

Enquiries can then be made about the kind of family life the
man is really wanting:
Can you help me understand what kind of family life you are now wanting?
How do you want it to be different from the way it was before?
What kind of changes would you like to make?
*What kind of changes do you think Jill/(the victim)/your kids would want
to see?*

Without endorsing family reunion, the therapist can invite the
man to clarify and extend his goals by means of "irresistible" invitations to
responsibility:
Do you want a family life which is healthy and satisfying for every member?
Do you want a family life in which there is no risk of abuse whatsoever?
*Do you want a family life where no one feels fearful or in any danger of
abuse?*
*Do you want a family that stays together out of love and respect for one
another or one that stays together because they feel they should - out of
obligation or because they are scared not to - out of fear?*

The man's arguments may be challenged in order to invite him
to give more consideration to his goals and weigh up previously
unrecognized choices and options more thoroughly:
*Are you sure? Plenty of men want to go back to exactly the way things were
in the past. Some haven't got the courage to try to make changes. Others
believe that it is their right - that it doesn't matter what other people's feelings
and needs are - what they want is most important.*

The man who has served a prison sentence may be invited to
draw comparisons between himself and extremely irresponsible men that
he has encountered:
You must have met men like that when you were inside?

In this way the therapist can invite the man to weigh up and establish whether he is wanting to move **forwards or backwards,** a choice he has probably not previously considered.

When the man is acknowledging the needs for safety, respect and change, the therapist can invite him to consider and clarify a new role for himself which will be helpful to all family members:

I understand that your family is extremely important to you and that you are wanting to go forwards not backwards. I agree that you have a vital role in helping resolve problems in your family, particularly after you have let them down in such a terrible way.

The therapist can help the man to clarify his role in assisting those he has victimized with invitations to responsibility which relate to the theme of **respect, trust and the welfare of family members**:

Do you think that (the victim)/Jill has lost some trust and respect for you as a result of your abuse?

If the man answers this question affirmatively, the therapist may invite him to take a giant step in facing up to his own shame and its consequences:

Have you lost some respect for yourself also?

Now the man can be invited to consider the impact of his abusive behaviour and the need for him to take action in the light of his goals and wishes for his family:

Is it important to you to try to regain/earn back the respect of (the victim)/Jill/your children? - Your own self-respect?

Do you want the kids/your partner to be able to see you as responsible and trustworthy?

Do you want this respect or trust to be real or just a pretence?

How would you like your kids to think of you/remember you when they are adults?

Do you want your kids to see you/talk to you out of duty and obligation or out of respect and love?

Do you want your wife to be with you out of duty and obligation or out of love and respect?

The therapist should acknowledge and highlight any steps the man has taken towards responsibility (e.g. acknowledgement of the abuse, moving out of the family home etc.), as evidence of the strength of his commitment to try to earn back respect.

Alan Jenkins

The man can be invited to clarify his responsibilities regarding the future **welfare of the children**:

Is it important to you that (the victim) carries as few scars of your abuse as possible into his/her adult life?

Is it important to you that s/he grows up to be a healthy independent adult man/woman?

Is it important to you that you help (the victim) to heal the scars of your sexual abuse?

Are you sure? Some men believe that helping and caring for kids is a mother's responsibility. Some men think that kids can get over anything and should just grow themselves up - its their problem.

Are you prepared to take full responsibility for your abuse or would you be prepared to leave some of the load on (the victim's) shoulders?

Are your prepared to take full responsibility for your abuse or would you settle for leaving up to Jill to try and sort out the mess?

If **intergenerational patterns** of abuse have been identified in the extended family, the man can be invited to attend to his role in stopping the "cycle":

Are you the first person in your family who has abused others but made a stand to try to stop it?

Do you want to stop the cycle of abuse that has been handed down from parents to children in your family?

How would you feel if your children carried on this tradition/followed in your footsteps?

Some men experience considerable difficulty in understanding and appreciating the need for change and for a new role in helping family members and they begin to dismiss the therapist's invitations and intensify arguments for the status quo. It is vital that the therapist understands restraints to these men accepting new responsibilities. The man may appear to be overwhelmed by his panic and desperation about the potential loss of his family. Another restraint relates to the man's **ignorance** about the nature of abuse, abuse-related trauma and its resolution. It can be helpful for the therapist to externalize this restraint and invite the man to hear new information to assist him in making his own decisions:

I understand clearly that you are desperate to get back into your family and help pick up the pieces. You made it clear to me that you want to help all members of your family to be able to put the abuse behind them. One thing

I am wondering is whether, in all the chaos and disruption that followed (the victim's) disclosure, anyone has taken the time to explain to you what is happening and what to expect - why this action is being taken and what effect the whole thing can have on the kids.

Often, in their haste to make sure the children are safe, welfare authorities can neglect the needs of the man who often has no idea of what is going on. Some authorities are only interested in apprehending and punishing the man and overlook his needs completely, especially the need for him to understand how he can try to put things right and make amends for what he has done.

The other thing I find with most men I meet is that while they understand that the abuse is illegal and wrong - they have no idea about how it can effect (the victim) and what s/he needs after having disclosed it. Many men, through not knowing this, find themselves going around in circles trying to help, getting more and more desperate:

Has anyone filled you in on what is happening? Has anyone ever talked to you about how sexual abuse can effect kids and how some of these effects can be prevented?

The therapist may proceed to ask whether the man would be interested in some explanations and in receiving some new information. I find it helpful to give explanations about the roles and processes of the welfare and legal systems and then to provide an explanation for some of the impacts and consequences of sexual abuse in a family context. In this way, the man can be helped to evaluate the need for a mission in responsibility to assist family members whom he has victimized.

It is useful to centre this explanation around the concept of **boundaries** in families. The term "boundary" reflects notions of separateness, privacy and rights to ones own property. Boundaries define what is public and what is "out of bounds". This term is easily understood and helps to clarify separate roles and rights of adults and children. I first warn the man about the challenging nature of this information and ask his permission for me to proceed:

Most men know that their abuse is illegal and wrong but very few men I meet know why it is dangerous, what harm it can do and how it can affect kids. This information is pretty difficult to hear and pretty challenging for men who have never really considered it. Can you handle some straight information that might hurt to listen to?

Alan Jenkins

I then introduce the notion of boundaries, sometimes with the aid of a family genogram drawn up on a whiteboard, and seek to make the following main points:

Boundaries are vital for kids to grow up to be healthy and independent. When children are babies their boundaries are really unclear - they don't see themselves as being separate persons from their parents. As they grow up they learn to see themselves more and more as separate persons and to make their own decisions and find out who they really are. A kid gradually learns to become his/her own person rather than remaining his/her parent's person. The boundaries which tell them who they are, get clearer and clearer as kids grow up.

Parents have a special role to help kids to grow to be really clear about their boundaries and to know which stuff is kid business and which stuff is adult business, so that their kids can find themselves and become their own persons. Your sexual abuse of (the victim) is one of the biggest violations of these boundaries that can happen. Instead of keeping your needs and your problems separate from (the victim's) you have got them muddled up with his/hers. You wound up dumping your adult business and problems in his/her lap.

You probably didn't mean it this way but in doing this you taught (the victim) to take on your adult business - your feelings and your problems on his/her shoulders. You taught (the victim) to think that they are his/her problems, to worry about your feelings and to keep your secrets. As you know, parents are supposed to look after kid's feelings and kid's needs but (the victim) wound up looking after your feelings and your needs. Kids can't learn to take care of their own business and their own growing up if they are burdened with adult business and carrying around an adult's problems - if they feel they have to worry about and look after you and your feelings.

However, this is only the beginning. Can you handle me going on? It takes some courage to face up to this.

At first, kids don't know that what they are getting into is wrong. They trust their parents completely. When the kid realises that something is wrong, however, they generally think it's his/her fault, that s/he is responsible. Some kids believe that they are bad and dirty and that they should never had let it happen. They are too young to realise that they are only little and that they were conned. Some kids privately come to see themselves as no good or completely worthless. They are not able to see what part of it is their business and what part of it is your business, like adults can.

This becomes very confusing. When the child realises that s/he has been taken advantage of by a person that s/he is supposed to be able to trust, then s/he wonders whether s/he can trust anyone. This can have devastating consequences for future relationships.

The therapist can proceed to detail other potential consequences to the child which appear relevant in the context of the man's abuse.

Throughout the explanation, the man is invited to consider his responsibilities in the light of his boundary violations, their impact on the victim and the child's tendency to accept responsibility for his abusive behaviour. The therapist can express respect for the man's preparedness to receive and consider new information which is both painful and challenging:

I believe it is important that you have all information at your disposal, even if this information is painful to hear, so that you can weigh up what is required of you at this time and whether you can handle it.

The man who has served a prison sentence and who protests that he has "paid his debt to society" and wants to return to his family, may be invited to examine the consequences of his prison sentence:

Did serving time help you in any way?
Did it help you understand or face what you did to (the victim)?
Did it help anyone in your family?

He will generally describe prison as a negative and unhelpful experience for all concerned. The therapist can acknowledge the fact that prison is often unhelpful and simply serves to put things that need to be addressed in a family on hold for a period of time. The only "debt" paid is the one to society. The man is then invited to attend to his goal of assisting his family:

Is it society you really wanted to pay a debt to or your family?
Is it society you wanted to put things right with or yourself and your family?

In these ways, the man is invited to consider one aspect of his **mission** which will involve facing up to and accepting full responsibility for his abuse, in order to help both the child and other family members to lift the burden of responsibility and shame that he has dumped on them. This is one step in a mission to help the child to be able to establish clear boundaries, throw off the legacy of abuse left by the man and be free to grow up to be an independent person. His mission is to communicate respect and responsibility and attempt to restore appropriate boundaries

Alan Jenkins

within the family, regardless of whether he ever returns to live in this context.

INVITATIONS TO PREVENT RECURRENCE OF THE ABUSE

The mission should also relate to the goal of preventing the reoccurrence of any further abuse against any person. This goal is equally relevant in situations where the victim(s) are family members or unrelated to the offender. Clearly, in the latter case, the man's mission in relieving the burden of responsibility for the child and demonstrating respect of appropriate boundaries may be less relevant.

The man may be invited to express his commitment to preventing any further abuse:

How important is it to you to know that you have taken every step you can to guarantee you will never abuse again?

What would it mean to you if you re-offended?

If the man argues that "it won't happen again", that he wants to "get on with my life" and that he is not sexually interested in children, the therapist should attend to the responsible aspects of the man's goals and help him to clarify these but decline his invitations to avoid addressing the abuse:

I understand that there is no way you want to find yourself back in a situation where you abuse another child and that you feel sure that there is no way that you will ever abuse again.

How did you come to this decision?

What makes you confident that you can achieve your goal?

I guess you have done a lot of thinking and soul-searching about this issue. Can you help me understand what you have realised about what you did?

What kind of plans have you made to prevent it every happening again?

Generally speaking, the man's explanations and answers to these questions will reflect a high degree of self-centredness like those representing denial of the likelihood of recurrence of the abuse listed in Figure 1. These explanations are based solely on hope and wishful thinking and they promote ineffective and misguided attempts to deal with the abuse. Very little thought is given to the impact of the abuse upon the child and there is little evidence of acceptance of responsibility.

I find it helpful to distinguish between the man's intent and his plan of action. Whilst his behaviour and thinking reflect a high level of avoidance of responsibility, he may genuinely believe that he will no longer offend. Any attempt to challenge this belief would be disrespectful and unhelpful:

I feel that I need to give you some information, particularly because I understand that you are sincere in wanting to put abuse behind you and get on with your life.

I believe that you are genuine and sincere in not wanting it to happen again and in believing that it won't happen again.

What concerns me is not your genuineness and sincerity but whether or not you have enough understanding and a plan which will work, to back up your good intentions.

The therapist may now ask the man's permission to provide him with further information to help him to externalize restraints to facing up and planning prevention strategies:

Can I give you some information that I have learned from working with other men in your situation.

Most men that I meet are terribly disturbed and distressed by what they did. Most regret it deeply. Most have felt disgusted with themselves. It is an extremely painful thing to face up to and think about. Most men wind up feeling more and more guilty, ashamed and rotten inside when they think about their abuse because they don't have ways to think about it which can lead to greater self-respect and inner strength. Do you know what I mean?

As they think about their abuse they generally feel worse and consequently they try to push it out of their minds and put it behind them. Most men try to do this too soon before they have fully understood how they got themselves into abusing a child. They have not yet faced up to it fully and have left stones unturned.

Another thing I have found is that when the abuse comes out into the open, most men do not experience any sexual interest in kids or thoughts of abusing them. This is especially the case when they are facing stressful legal proceedings and family problems.

If stones have been left unturned and you don't have a full understanding, then there is a high risk of abuse sticking its nose into your business again, in spite of your good intentions. Many men have found themselves ambushed by thoughts and feelings they thought they had finished with long ago and get sucked back in to abusing before they have realised what is happening.

The man is then invited to consider new criteria for evaluating his likelihood of reoffending and determining the need to plan prevention strategies:

The only way you can know that your beliefs are grounded in fact rather than in hope is when you know that you have faced up to all aspects of the abuse and you understood it completely.

The best way of making this judgement for yourself is to ask yourself three questions:

Firstly, can you handle thinking and talking about what happened - really facing it, or are your feelings of guilt and shame in charge and keeping you on the run from it?

Can you think and talk about the abuse and begin to feel the inner strength that comes with knowing that you can face these feelings of guilt and shame - that they are not in charge and dictating to you what you should do?

Can you face them or are you still on the run from them and trying to avoid them?

Secondly, do you understand how you got yourself into abusing (the victim) in the first place?

Did you anticipate it/did you feel it coming before it happened or did you find yourself caught up in it and unable to stop it before you realised it was happening?

How do you know it couldn't sneak up on you again?

Thirdly, do you have a good understanding of what you have put (the victim) and others through?

Did you intend to use/hurt/betray (the victim) or was it more the case that you didn't think of or consider (the victim's) feelings and how your abuse could affect him/her?

What have you done to become a more sensitive and understanding person? What have you done to fill the gaps in your understanding and sensitivity?

Most men who abuse others were not intending to hurt them but were generally caught up in their own feelings and quite insensitive to the feelings and needs of the other person at the time. Until you have filled this gap in your understanding you are not ready to put the incidents behind you.

I believe that you are genuine. That is why I think it is wise for you to have all the information at your disposal so that you can make a judgement as to whether your beliefs are based on hope and good intentions or a solid grounding of understanding; so that you know that you are in charge of the future and not just a slave to your fears and your feelings of shame and guilt.

INVITATIONS TO SELF-RESPECT AND INTEGRITY

When the man acknowledges a loss of self-respect, as a result of his abusive actions, the therapist may invite him to consider his mission as a medium for earning or establishing self-respect, self-confidence and a new sense of integrity:

Is it important for you to try to earn back your self-respect?

How important is this for you and your future goals?

What would it mean for you and your future goals if you didn't try?

What do you think you will need to do?

What difference would facing up or copping out make?

Which would lead to genuine self-respect and which would lead to more pretence?

Are you prepared to earn self-respect the hard way by facing the painful consequences of your actions or could you pull the wool over your eyes and ride along on unearned sympathy and forgiveness from others?

The man's arguments for responsibility and for engaging in a mission in responsibility provide a point of reference, based on his goals, to which the therapist can return throughout therapy to assist in considering and evaluating plans and actions. These arguments are not regarded as evidence of responsibility or of readiness to take new steps but as statements of commitment to new action.

Alan Jenkins

INVITE THE MAN TO CONSIDER HIS READINESS TO EMBARK ON A MISSION IN RESPONSIBILITY

If the man is arguing for a mission in responsibility, he may be invited to plan specific details of this mission, consider his readiness to embark upon it and prepare himself for an extremely challenging journey.

Whether the mission is initially centred around the goal of contributing to the child's welfare and healing or the goals of preventing any further abuse and promoting self-respect, the man will need to carefully consider the steps that he plans to take and his readiness to handle what is required of him.

The man who argues for an active role in helping the victim may have expressed that he accepts full responsibility and that he wants to help the victim to understand this. He may prematurely believe that he is ready to make an apology to the victim. The therapist can invite him to examine more closely the requirements of this task and to assess his readiness to take action:

In order to achieve this you will need to look very closely at what you have put (the victim) and others through, and not only think but feel about what it would be like to be in their shoes, and the ways that your abuse could affect them both now and in the future. I feel I should warn you that this is an extremely painful and challenging task.

If you tried to apologise and get your message of responsibility across to (the victim) without understanding at all what it would be like to be in his/her shoes - what do you think your apology would mean?

What message do you think it would give (the victim) about you?

Do you think it would help or harm?

Do you think it would lead to greater respect or disrespect?

Do you think (the victim) would think you are serious and genuine or just looking for the easy way out?

You will need to try to understand what you have put others through and the effects this could have on them before you can be of any help. Can you handle the prospect of facing that?

How important is it for you to try to help lift your burden from (the victim's) shoulders?

How important is it for you to try to earn back (the victim's) respect?

How necessary do you think it is to try to understand (the victim's) experience?

It will mean taking a really close look at your abuse - something that most men try to avoid or run away from. Most men try to put it behind them before they have even faced up to it. Do you think you can handle facing it?

The therapist may then help the man to detail each of the specific steps which constitute his mission. A typical set of such steps is presented in Appendix I.

The man can be invited to consider each of these steps:

It sounds like you understand clearly that you have a vital mission to take responsibility for your abuse. This means being able to face up to and acknowledge the full extent of your abuse, even though this will hurt. It means being able to take full responsibility - so that (the victim) no longer carries your responsibilities for you and faces your problems for you.

THE ISSUE OF DISTANCE/SEPARATENESS - MOVING OUT OF THE HOME

I often find it helpful to reintroduce the notion of boundaries at this point and invite the man to consider the decision to move out of the family home (if the child is a family member) or to take an active role in initiating and maintaining distance or separateness from the child. If welfare or parole authorities have already instigated this separateness, I invite the man to take an active role in this process rather than regard himself as a passive and powerless victim of a welfare state. Establishing and respecting distance and separateness are promoted as **active** steps in taking responsibility for abuse.

The man may present in an angry and desperate state and regard welfare or parole authorities as having kicked him out of his home and as preventing him from seeing his family. One such man, in his desperate but insensitive attempts to "help", defied the welfare authorities and regularly transported his daughter to her counselling appointments.

Alan Jenkins

These men are invited to take an active but sensitive role in contributing to distance and separateness:

Most men don't understand the reasons that welfare advise separation. They think it is only for the safety of the child and many feel clear that they won't abuse again. Consequently, they don't see any point in moving out of the home. In fact, many men worry that it might be destructive because they want to be in there helping. They feel that living out of the home stops them from being able to do anything and they feel helpless because they think that there is nothing they can do until this time is over.

Most men think the best way to help would be to get in there straight away and try to reassure (the victim) and try to get close - to try to show (the victim) that it won't happen again.

Most men don't have the information they need to able to make the best decision on this matter and many find themselves going around and around in circles. They don't realise getting apart actually achieves a lot more than just the physical safety of the child. In fact it is one of the most important steps of all in helping the victim get over the abuse and throw off responsibility for it.

Do you understand how it could help in this way?

The man is invited to participate in discussion and decisions regarding separation rather than passively accept it as an external imposition:

I believe that it is a decision that should not just be left up to welfare or the police but one that you should have an active role in understanding and in making. I believe welfare should only force decisions when men don't take responsibility themselves. However, you need all the information to be able to make a wise decision for yourself.

The therapist may then ask the man's permission to provide him with relevant information. I find it useful to return to explanations of boundaries, when explaining the need for separation:

When you abused (the victim) you violated his/her personal boundaries and betrayed his/her trust in one of the worst possible ways. One of the hardest things to understand is that possibly the worst thing you could do at this time would be to make contact and try to reassure (the victim). Your intentions would be excellent but it would only cause confusion for (the victim).

Distance is vital. It not only makes sure its safe but it gives everybody space and time to consider their own feelings. When you abused (the victim) you messed up his/her boundaries and taught him/her to worry about your feelings and your needs rather than the his/her own. You probably didn't mean it but you taught (the victim) to take responsibility for you and your problems. (The victim) needs time and space to be helped to get clear on what are his/her problems and what are your problems. If you came back into the family now, (the victim) might feel s/he had to worry about your feelings again - not just whether it might happen again but how you are getting on and how s/he could help you. What you have helped me understand is that after having realised how badly you have let (the victim) down, leaned on, and taught (the victim) to carry your problems and your responsibilities, you now want to help him/her to throw this burden off not take it on again.

What do you think it would mean if you went back in the family and (the victim) started to worry more about your feelings than his/her own - just like before?

What would this do for (the victim)?

What if you went home and this action prompted welfare to remove (the victim) - what message would it give him/her about who is responsible?

What action would be most likely to ensure that (the victim) feels no pressure or worry about further abuse, keeping secrets for you, keeping feelings to him/herself, feeling responsible for the above?

You let them down through actions that were wrong and now you need to show them in actions that you are serious about taking responsibility - that you care enough to give them the space - that you care enough to put their needs first and your needs second. Your actions will speak far louder than any words.

Are you fully prepared to put (the victim's) needs before your own?

Moving out not only gives a loud and clear message to everyone that you are taking responsibility and that you are putting others' needs first but also helps (the victim) to set new boundaries. It says that you recognise that you are both separate people and it guarantees that there is no way (the victim) can get his/her needs muddled up with yours or that you can get yours muddled up with theirs.

The man may argue that the child is missing him and is indicating that s/he wants him home. The therapist can agree that it is likely that the child will miss the man, particularly if he has occupied a parental role. This is a time, however, for the man to stand firm and take the lead:

This is not a time to let a child make the decisions. (The victim) has had to carry too much responsibility already and will be confused and trying to decide what's best for everybody. This is a time when (the victim) will need strong leadership from you and Jill. You need to weigh up what is best and make a stand for what you believe will be most helpful for (the victim's) future.

The man may also be preoccupied with the length of time that "he is required" to live separately from his family. The therapist can respond:

It is not the length of time that is important but what you do in that time to face up and try to earn back respect.

I generally invite the man to take the initiative by setting a measured pace and by trying not to rush others into premature reunion:

If you go at a steady pace and avoid trying to hurry your family, what message do you think it will give them?

If you try to rush in, what message do you think it will give them? - Will they think you are considering and understanding their needs or just thinking of your own needs?

Do you think they will think you have changed? - that you can put their feelings first or that you still are putting your own feelings before theirs?

The therapist may invite the man to examine his own resources and further challenge his readiness to act on his mission:

This is only one of a number of tough decisions that you will need to face. Do you think you are ready?

What tells you that you are ready?

What tough decisions have you already faced?

What strong actions have you already taken?

How will you handle your fears and insecure feelings at not seeing (the victim) and not knowing what is happening with (the victim)?

How will you handle the challenge of not living at home and of facing the pressures of a whole new lifestyle?

What tells you that you can handle these pressures and challenges?

How have you handled them so far?

It will be extremely challenging. It may be the toughest thing you have ever tried to do. I feel that I should warn you that you will feel a lot worse before you will begin to feel better. You have been unable to face up to it previously because it has made you feel so bad. In fact, you will feel so desperate at times you may feel like quitting.

I would understand if you want to pull out - if you don't think you can handle it.

IMPLEMENTING THE MISSION PART 1 -FACING THE ABUSE

The following are presented as a sequence of overlapping steps. The man will be working on several of them simultaneously, returning to extend or complete former steps while working on steps later in the sequence. The process of engagement is applied to each step as the man is invited to face a new responsibility, externalize restraints, plan new actions and discover new abilities and capacities in himself.

ACKNOWLEDGEMENT OF THE ABUSE

The therapist initially invites the man to acknowledge the full extent of his abuse and to face and discuss it in full detail. This is an extremely challenging step which can be distressing for both the man and the therapist. The man is invited to "take an honest look" at the details of his abuse, to "look it squarely in the eye" without "running away from it" and to face up to the feelings of shame, guilt and embarrassment which will accompany this process.

Before commencing this step, the man is invited to prepare himself for what will be a painful and challenging task. The therapist can help him to develop a context for understanding the significance of this step - to consider the reasons for taking it and to clarify how it will help him and others. He may be invited to consider the significance of this step in the context of his goal to assist the victim:

Could you take yourself seriously - or would you be kidding yourself, if you thought you could understand what you have put (the victim) through, without facing the details of what you actually did to him/her?

Do you think you could ever hope to understand (the victim's) feelings if you never looked closely at what you did to him/her?

What would it mean to you if (the victim) faced up to more of the details of your abuse than you did?

The man may also be invited to consider the significance of facing the details of his abuse in the context of his goal to prevent further abuse:

One of the reasons that many men are unable to take charge of and stop their abusive behaviour, is that they have always avoided thinking about it. When they do, they feel ashamed, guilty and worried, and they can't handle it. Consequently, they block it out of their minds or learn to justify it to themselves. The man doesn't think about it and leaves it up to the child to do the worrying and to take responsibility to try to stop it. This means that the child is often quite clear about the details of what happened and how the abuse developed. The man, on the other hand has never taken a close look at it and can't organise himself to stop it let alone understand how it developed and what is keeping it going. He learns to pull the wool over his own eyes - to kid himself and pretend it isn't a problem or that it isn't really doing any harm.

If you never took a close look at what you did to (the victim), do you think you would ever understand how you started to abuse and how you kept it going?

Do you think you could ever feel 100% sure that you understood it fully and it would never happen again?

I find it helpful to establish a **context of strength and self-respect** for the man to face his feelings of shame and guilt which are initially restraints to facing up. This commences with a warning:

I feel I should warn you before you begin. If you begin to honestly face up to your abuse you will probably find it one of the most painful things you have ever done. It will mean facing feelings of shame and guilt and initially feeling terrible inside. These feelings will get worse before they get better.

I generally explain the notion of **"inner strength"** which is developed when a man faces difficult or challenging pressures in his life. The process of facing up works on the principle of "no pain no gain." Metaphors about the development of physical fitness, following regular, sustained and often painful physical activity, may be used on to illustrate the notion that feelings of inner strength are preceded by the painful experience of facing shame, guilt and the details of abuse:

Do you think it would be possible to develop inner strength without facing painful truths?

If you were able to face up to the details of what you did and the shame that will accompany it, what would this say about you?

Alan Jenkins

If you failed to face up to it and ran away from it or copped out - what would this say about you?

What would this mean for your future?

What would this tell others about you?

What would it mean if you left it up to (the victim) to face the painful truths of your abuse and tried to bury your head in the sand?

The man is invited to reaffirm his commitment to the task and his readiness to commence. He is then encouraged to proceed at his own pace. It is vital that the man argues for the commencement of the task, not the therapist.

The therapist should also acknowledge steps the man has already taken which are consistent with the process of facing up to his abuse. He is invited to access his own courage and the resources used in taking these steps:

How did you find the courage to acknowledge the abuse when your wife confronted you?

You must have felt like copping out or denying it?

How did you find the courage to face up to it?

What difference has it made to you/to your self-respect?

The therapist may proceed to ask **detailed behavioural questions** to facilitate the man facing up to his abuse. These questions ask details of Who? When? Where? and What?, but avoid invitations to the man to speculate about Why? Examples of such questions are presented in Appendix II.

I find it helpful to use clear and unambiguous language, from the commencement of therapy, in order to help the man label his behaviour appropriately. For example, I refrain from using words like "fondling" or "interfering with" but label the behaviour as "sexual abuse" and invite the man to do likewise. The wording of questions can help the man to attend to the coercion and deception that is inherent in his abusive behaviour. The question, *How did you trick (the victim) into abuse?* may initially lead to protestations by the man that he didn't trick his victim - s/he was willing. He can, however, be invited to accept the label, "trick", if challenged to attend to details of the ways in which he gradually introduced sexual behaviour into games and interaction with the child, the ways in which he encouraged the child to think that the abuse was acceptable behaviour and incentives and enticements offered to the child for participation in the abuse.

The specific behavioural questions also examine ways in which the man set the child up to take responsibility for his abusive behaviour. He is invited to attend to the methods of deception, mentioned above, as well as the ways that he encouraged the child to set limits on and initiate sexual behaviour, threats and appeals to the child's guilt and explanations or justifications given to the child.

As the man faces details of his abusive behaviour, he is frequently invited to attribute meaning and significance to this process by attending to the courage he is showing in searching out the truth. The steps he takes are highlighted as significant in relation to his goals. The therapist may invite him to notice any feelings of inner strength associated with facing up as well as inevitable feelings of discomfort and distress.

I often encourage the man to write or tape record the detailed story of his abuse, in order to create a permanent record which can greatly assist the process of facing up. This is generally an ongoing project which the man adds to over time as he faces up to more detail. He is encouraged to understand the value of looking at details of his abuse in "black and white" because this is a harder step than simply thinking or talking about them. I invite the man to read his story out loud during appointments and attend to the development of inner strength and self-respect that these steps facilitate.

Written tasks provide an opportunity for the therapist to invite the man to evaluate the current influence of restraining habits of avoidance of responsibility for the abuse, in his life. I generally spend considerable time enquiring about the nature and significance of the man's experience, whilst attempting to engage in and completing the task:

How did putting it down in black and white affect you?

How did you handle your guilt/shame, etc?

How did you approach the task? - Did you get straight into it/put it off until the last moment/night before your appointment?

Did you let yourself get into it or did you give in to old habits of copping out, forgetting, procrastinating, etc?

What effect has it had on you? What difference has it made? In what ways has it helped you? Was it worth the pain and struggle?

What does it say about you that you completed such a task?

As the man begins to acknowledge his abuse to a wider audience, particularly family members and other significant persons, he is invited to attend to the significance and meaning of these steps; in particular, the impact of the breaking of oppressive family secrets, the correct attribution of responsibility and the personal risk involved in increasing the extent of his facing up:

What does this say about you - about your level of responsibility?
What message does it give to others?

Many men are surprised when others respect such risk-taking and are supportive; that others can recognise the sincerity and integrity which underlies genuine facing up as opposed to taking a condemnatory and rejecting stance.

It is vital that the therapist has an account of the child's version of events, in order to corroborate the man's story. Most men significantly understate the frequency and nature of their abuse and are vague about details at first. Over time, the man can be invited to face up to the full extent of his abuse and attend to discrepancies between his and the child's versions of events. Over the course of therapy, the man may offer considerably more details of the abuse than occurs in the child's account of events (much to the chagrin of some solicitors!) and sometimes abuse of other persons is revealed.

If the therapeutic context is perceived by the man as respectful one, the therapist can become increasingly confronting over time. However, extended facing up is generally facilitated by direct and specific questions, written exercises and the therapist communicating respect for each new step the man takes.

In early sessions I generally try to set an expectation of further facing up to details at the next appointment, especially when there are large discrepancies between the man's and the victim's accounts of the abuse. This involves externalisation of restraints to facing up by further acknowledgment of the man's fears and feelings of shame and his tendency to push this experience out of awareness. The therapist may also acknowledge that when the man thinks about the abuse, it may not seem "real". It may feel like he was "another person". It may feel out of character for him. At times when he abused he may have felt "like in a dream." The therapist acknowledges that these factors lead to many men trying to forget the abuse and "push it right to the backs of their minds". They may do this to such an extent that they **temporarily forget** details. The therapist may add that this is a short term phenomenon and that as the man faces up and thinks more about his abuse he will recall more and more detail over time. He is told that he does not have to acknowledge everything at once and that other details **will** come to his mind and that he **will** gradually remember more clearly. In this way, the man is provided with a face-saving way out of early denial and is assisted to organise the timing and process of his own facing up.

In later sessions, if the theraputic context is perceived by the man as a respectful one, the therapist can directly confront the man about discrepancies between his and the child's account of events. Initially, many men are preoccupied with the "real truth" about what actually took place and self-righteously claim that the child was mistaken about minor details of the abuse.

The man may be invited to question the value of pursuing the exact truth, in the context of his mission of responsibility. He may be invited to consider the significance of such discrepancies in the light of the fact that the child believes that these events took place. If he is vague or "can't remember" what happened, he is encouraged to consider where the benefit of the doubt should lie, in the context of his mission. If he is hazy about events, he may be asked whether he is prepared to rely on the child's memory and let him/her take responsibility for his facing up or whether he believes he should extend himself and do his own facing up?

When attending to the child's perceptions of events, as opposed to the "truth", the man may be invited to consider the significance and consequences of attempts to challenge the child's story:

If you challenge (the victim's) account, what will this mean for (the victim) if s/he believes that this is what really happened?

Where would this leave (the victim)/other family members?

What message would it give regarding who is taking responsibility?

What consequences would this have for (the victim) - in the courtroom - in your family - for the child's wellbeing?

Would (the victim)/others think you were facing responsibility or copping out?

Do you think you would be facing up or copping out?

The man who protests that his abusive behaviour was an accident or that his intentions were misinterpreted, may be invited to consider his responsibilities according to his mission. The therapist can point out that the child believes that s/he was abused by the man. The man is invited to consider what this means in terms of adult-child boundaries; that the child is not convinced that the man respects the privacy of his/her body and not convinced that he respects clear adult-child boundaries. He may be invited to consider:

Who is responsible for making sure that children feel respected by adults?
Whose job is it to see that a child feels secure and safe with an adult?
Whose job is it set clear and safe adult-child boundaries?

In this way, the man is invited to take responsibility for having acted in a way that led the victim to feel abused. He is invited to take responsibility to acknowledge the consequences of his actions, and acknowledge that he has not acted clearly enough, over the long term, to convince the child that he respects appropriate boundaries.

The man may then be asked:

Did you anticipate that (the victim) would react/see it in this way?

The answer to this question raises the possibility that the man has a **bigger problem than just being the child's abuser**, particularly if other children have also felt abused by him. Does he have a tendency to be unaware of the impact of his actions upon others? Does this mean that other children are likely to feel abused by him while he remains unaware of it? Does this mean that this man is a danger in the community? It may be simpler and better for him to face up to the allegations of abuse.

ACCEPTING FULL RESPONSIBILITY FOR THE ABUSE

Inviting the man to acknowledge the significance of his abuse

Most men understate or minimise the seriousness of their abusive actions and the potential they have to cause both short and long term distress to the child and others. When such actions are acknowledged, they are generally not labelled as abuse, particularly if they do not involve penis penetration. The use of terms such as "fondling", "interfering", "fiddling", "touching up" etc, contribute to mislabelling and minimization of the seriousness of sexual abuse. (Typical explanations and justifications are presented in Figure 1.) Abusive sexual behaviour is often confused with love or caring, education of the child and even parental rights. Participation of the child which is achieved through coercion and deception can be mistaken to be informed consent. Roles, responsibilities and expectations of children and adults are frequently confused.

The man can attend to the significance and seriousness of his abusive behaviour if he is invited to face up to exact details of his actions and educated about differentials in age, power, knowledge and responsibility which exists between adults and children. He can be helped to understand differences existing between adults and children in thinking, experience, dependency, vulnerability, naivety, ease of intimidation, maturity and tendency to accept responsibility.

A typical presentation which illustrates understatement of the significance of abuse, is the man who protests that the child is showing "no ill effects", is acting "in a loving and caring way", "comes up for cuddles" or "acts no differently towards me." I find it helpful to invite him to consider the child's behaviour in the wider context of patterns of family loyalty and dependency. It is particularly helpful to draw the distinction between the child's attempts to deal with the abuse and the child's feelings of loyalty and caring towards the man:

It is clear that (the victim) cares about you/loves you/is loyal to you.
What is not clear is how s/he is dealing with the consequences of your abuse.

The therapist may then enquire about any evidence of trauma which the man or others have noticed:

Has (the victim) shown any signs of distress/betrayal/feeling let down by you? - at any other time? - to others? - would you know if she had?

The man may then be invited to "put himself in the shoes of the victim" and speculate about the child's rights and entitlements:

Do you think that (the victim) feels mostly angry or mostly guilty about your abuse of him/her?
"Which feeling do you think is a more healthy one for (the victim)?
Do you think that (the victim) is entitled to feel betrayed/used/let down by you?
How would you feel, if you were in (the victim's) shoes?

These questions may be particularly challenging for the man who will generally acknowledge the child's entitlement to feel used and betrayed by him. He may then be invited to speculate as to the reasons why the child does not display feelings to which s/he is clearly entitled:

Do you think that (the victim) does not feel let down/betrayed/used at all or do you think that (the victim) feels these feelings but doesn't show them?

Either way the man answers, he is asked to attribute meaning and significance to the child's behaviour and to consider his responsibility in the light of this.

For example, if he believes that the child does not feel let down or betrayed:

Alan Jenkins

What do you think that means?

Do you think (the victim) has thought deeply about it and believes that what you did is OK?

or

Do you think that (the victim) does not feel able to look at your abuse of him/her for what it really is?

Alternatively, if he believes that the child feels let down and betrayed but doesn't show it:

What do you think that means?

Do you think that (the victim) is scared to express what s/he feels and thinks, or do you think that (the victim) is worried for you and believes that you couldn't handle it if s/he expressed his/her true feelings?

The man can now be invited to consider his responsibility in the light of his beliefs and speculations.

If he believes that the child thinks his abuse of him/her was OK:

What will that mean for (the victim's) future?

Do you want (the victim) to go on thinking that?

What do you want to do to correct (the victim's) misunderstanding?

How could you get that message across?

If he believes that the child does not feel able to look at the abuse for what it really is:

What will that mean for (the victim's) future?

If the man thinks that the child is scared to express feelings or thinks that the child believes that he couldn't handle their expression, then in a similar way, he can be asked to consider what each of these would mean for future of the child and what his responsibility is in each case.

It may also be helpful to ask the man's permission to give him information about the ways in which children cope with the aftermath of abuse. The therapist may draw attention to the facts that;

- ---------- abused children can simultaneously feel both betrayal and anger **and** loyalty, caring and love;
- ---------- victims of abuse are taught or trained to look after the abuser's feelings and to keep the abuse and any distress associated with it secret from all family members;
- ---------- victims of abuse become very adept at taking responsibility for the abuse and protecting the abuser and his feelings;

---------- sexual abuse victims frequently develop survival mechanisms based on denial, avoidance, and pretence, in order to deal with their own feelings of powerlessness and entrapment. These survival mechanisms are not too dissimilar from those deployed by the man himself.

He may be invited to consider that it is a healthy sign for the child to experience and express feelings of betrayal and anger as well as loving or caring feelings. It is interpreted as evidence that the child is dealing with and working through the abuse rather than avoiding or denying it:

Do you think it would be better if (the victim) could face the abuse now and deal with his/her feelings or would it be better for (the victim) to leave it unresolved and face the prospect of it affecting his/her life well into the future?

The man can then be invited to consider his role in helping the child to feel safe and entitled to express these feelings:

I understand that you believe that (the victim) is entitled to feel angry and betrayed?

Could you handle it if (the victim) showed these feelings in your presence? How could you get the message across that:

- you believed that (the victim) is entitled to these feelings?

- you don't need (the victim) to worry about your feelings?

- you can handle it if (the victim) expresses how s/he really feels?

The therapist should advise caution here and warn the man against approaching the child and telling him/her what to think and feel. This message is best communicated through actions rather than words. If the man believes in the child's entitlement and is prepared to handle the truth, then the child will get the message.

Another way that the man may attempt to minimise the significance of the abuse is to claim that the child enjoyed it and that he did not use physical force or coercion. He is then invited to consider the coercion and deception which are inherent in an adult's abuse of a child, given the differential in roles and responsibilities. He may also be invited to consider the likelihood that the child may experience even greater trauma and problems under these circumstances. A greater degree of guilt and shame and an increased sense of responsibility for the abuse may be experienced if the child later feels that participation was willing and should have been avoided. In this context, the man may need to consider a very active role in taking responsibility.

It is wise for the man to take a preventive stance, if he is uncertain about the presence or absence of ill effects of the abuse. It is evident that many children experience long term distress and consequences which are not always evident at the time of the abuse. In order to be sure that such consequences are minimised, the man should err on the side of safety rather than risk making a false assumption that the abuse has had no impact.

Inviting the man to accept full responsibility for his abuse

The man may acknowledge that his abuse is serious but disclaim responsibility for his actions and blame others or external events.

If the abuse is attributed to factors such as alcohol or marital problems, the man may be invited to attend to his responsibility for facing these problems:

What steps did you take to deal with your drinking when you associated it with your abuse of (the victim)?

What steps did you take to make sure you didn't drink when you were going to be in contact with (the victim)?

What steps did you take to address your marital/sexual problems?

What steps did you take to make sure that you were addressing these problems in a responsible way rather than taking them out on innocent people?

The man who protests that he was "asleep" or that he "didn't realise what I was doing" may be invited to consider two options, one which is developed as a "worse option" and seen clearly as undesirable.

The first option is presented as the most likely option - that the man has a facing up problem and he is not yet ready to acknowledge and attend to his abusive behaviour.

The second option - it is just possible that the man has a problem whereby he acts without realising what he is doing. The therapist should express concern and hope that this second option is not the case because this would mean a **very** serious problem exists. It would mean that the man could molest anyone in future without realising it - that he could not even anticipate this happening and therefore could not prevent it. The therapist may raise doubts that legal and welfare systems would feel confident about the man having any contact with children or even being loose in the community. This option would require much more frequent, complex and involved treatment.

In this way, the man may be invited to consider the easier option to face up to his abuse.

The man who attributes responsibility to the child will generally describe the child's behaviour as "provocative" and believe that s/he "enjoyed it", "initiated it" and behaved "seductively." He may be invited to challenge these perceptions in three ways;

---------- Firstly, the child's motivation is quite irrelevant He may be asked to consider what his responsibility is when a child behaves irresponsibly or inappropriately in his presence.

What should a parent/adult do in this case?

What is your responsibility in this case?

How did you approach this responsibility?

---------- Secondly, the therapist may help the man to understand his tendency to misinterpret and mislabel the behaviour of children. Young children are not able to draw mature distinctions between sexual and affectionate behaviour. They rapidly learn which behaviour gets closeness, affection and attention from adults. Adults who do not understand this misinterpret and attribute adult motives to children's behaviour.

Do you think (the victim) was wanting sex from you or love/affection/attention?

---------- Thirdly, the man may be invited to consider, in the light of his attempts to face up to the details of his abuse, how he has trained and shaped the child's behaviour towards participation in sexual activity, over a period of time.

In what ways did you give (the victim) the message that sexual behaviour with you was OK?

In what ways did you gradually shape (the victim's) behaviour in this direction over time?

How did you teach (the victim) to use sex in order to relate to you?

Inviting the man to acknowledge the need to take action to prevent further abuse.

In order to take full responsibility for the abuse, the man must acknowledge that it is a problem which is likely to recur unless faced up

Alan Jenkins

to it completely. This issue has previously been addressed in Step 2. However, the man may continue to express explanations and justifications which reflect denial of the likelihood of reoccurrence of abuse.

This is particularly relevant if the man claims that "it just happened once" and implies that he has nothing to worry about. The therapist can respond that it is rare for abuse to happen just once, particularly without any lead up or anticipation. The man may be asked:

Did you see it coming?

Did you anticipate the abuse?

"Did you have any thoughts or experience any signs or indications that you might sexually abuse (the victim)?

These questions create a bind for the man. If he responds that he did anticipate the abuse, then it would seem that he deliberately let it happen or was not in control of his actions. If he denies any anticipation, then the therapist may enquire:

How can you be sure that it won't happen again?

How can you say with 100% confidence that you could not be a risk to children again in the future?

The man who has offended over a period of time is invited to consider his previous pattern of reliance on others, especially the child, to take responsibility for the abuse:

What steps did you take to try to stop or prevent the abuse?

What stopped you from succeeding?

Who did take responsibility to avoid/prevent/stop it?

Are you prepared to rely on others to prevent further abuse or are you prepared to stand on your own feet?

What will you need to do to demonstrate to yourself that you can stand on your own two feet?

The therapist may then proceed to help the man to understand criteria for evaluating the risk of recurrence and the need for further work in facing responsibility, as outlined in Step 2.

RESPECTING DISTANCE AND SPACE FOR THE VICTIM AND OTHERS

I have previously discussed the process of inviting the man's active participation in distancing himself from the victim as a vital aspect of his mission in responsibility (see page). This generally involves the man agreeing to move out of the family home, if the child is a family member.

The man is also invited to consider how space and distance can be helpful to other family members. He may not have considered his partner's requirements for space and time in order to deal with her feelings of betrayal and grief. Like the spouse abuser, he may feel overwhelmed by feelings of insecurity and desperation, preoccupied with attempts to establish as much contact with his partner as he can and desperate to convince her to overlook the abuse and stay with him.

The man can be invited to understand how distance and space may help him as well as the child and other family members. Separation and distancing are particularly helpful in challenging patterns of dependency and reliance in family relationships. The man can be invited to consider his high level of reliance on the child to take responsibility for his feelings and for the abuse along with his high level of reliance on his partner. He can speculate about gains he might achieve by becoming more self-reliant and "standing on his own two feet":

When you look back on your period of separation from your family, what things do you think you will notice that you have gained yourself - things that you won't probably notice now while you are in a state of desperation?

If you are able to stand up to your desperate need to get back together with/see (the victim), what do you think you will stand to gain for yourself?

Do you see any advantage in becoming a more independent person - someone who can stand on his own two feet, or would it be better to stay reliant and be propped up by other family members?

It may useful to invite the man to take some responsibility for providing an explanation to the child, about his absence from the family; to take responsibility for explaining why he has moved out, why he is not having contact and who is responsible for this is consistent with his mission. It is generally best if this message is delivered by his partner or a counsellor working with the child, in order to avoid adverse effects of personal contact between the child and the man. The man can take responsibility for the message by writing a letter which can be read or given to the child.

If the man understands the value of, and agrees to participate in establishing distance and space, rather than passively complying with welfare directions, then he may be invited to consider the value of sending a message to the child:

If (the victim) believes that s/he is responsible for you moving out because s/he told someone about your abuse, what will this mean about the level of responsibility s/he will carry on his/her shoulders?
If (the victim) thinks that the welfare kicked you out, how could this affect his/her beliefs about who you think is responsible for the abuse?

The man is then invited to consider the kind of message he would like to send to the child. Even if the child or other family members do not want such a message to be delivered, it is still a useful step that can be taken by the man to accept full responsibility for his abuse:

What would you like (the victim) to understand about the reasons you are no longer living in the family?
Would you be prepared to leave this responsibility fully up to your partner and rely on her to deal with it or do you think it is appropriate that you take the responsibility yourself?

In this way, the man is invited to take responsibility for distance and space, to communicate that he is responsible for his abuse and to make it clear that it is his own decision to leave the family home. He may explain that he needs to do this in order to receive help so that he can learn to stop his abusive behaviour and learn to behave respectfully with children, as a father should.

The man can also be invited to attend to feelings of responsibility that the child may carry for his moving out, as a result of disclosing the abuse:

How do you think (the victim) might feel about having told about the abuse?
How would you like (the victim) to think about the fact that she told someone?

In this way he can be invited to help the child to understand that he believes s/he did the right thing in telling.

UNDERSTANDING THE IMPACT OF THE ABUSE

Once the man has acknowledged details of his abuse and accepts that it is his responsibility, he may be invited to consider more fully the potential impact of his actions upon the child and other family members. This requires that he **try** to "put himself into the shoes of" the child and other family members and to **try** understand what he has put them through and what they will have to contend with in the future, as a result of his abuse.

The failure of the man to comprehend and understand the destructive impact of his abusive behaviour, is a major restraint to him accepting full responsibility. Most sexual offenders understand that their abusive behaviour is illegal and morally wrong but remain quite insensitive to other's feelings and reactions during and after it has ceased. This lack of sensitivity and empathy is the other side of the man's high level of self-centeredness and self-preoccupation. Consequently, it makes it possible for the abuse to be justified and rationalized and for the child's and other's feelings to be ignored or overlooked.

To understand the impact is vital if the man is to cease his abuse and help the child and others deal with its aftermath. The man must be able to "feel for" what he has put the child through, in order to become a more sensitive and respectful person who will no longer take advantage of or harm others. I sometimes notice a shift in the man's pattern of remorse when he begins to understand the potential impact of his actions. The initial self-centered preoccupations with his own losses, hurts and fears may yield to remorse which is based more on feelings associated with a new awareness of the losses and hurts that he has inflicted upon others. At this point, he may be "feeling for" what he has done to the child and others rather than thinking intellectually about it.

The success of the man's mission pivots on this task of understanding the impact. An apology or attempt to help lift the child's burden of responsibility or contribution to the child's welfare would be meaningless in the absence of this understanding. The goals to prevent further abuse, earn genuine self-respect and develop sensitive and respectful relationships with others would also be impossible to achieve. If the man has not filled the gaps in his sensitivity and empathy then he has not fully faced the consequences of his own abuse.

This is the most challenging in the man's mission. If he truly faces the potential impact of his abusive actions then he will feel considerable despair as he faces his deepest shame. Once he has faced this the shame, he will grieve deeply for the hurts and losses that he has inflicted upon others.

This step requires considerable preparation:

---------   Firstly, the man must understand the importance of this task to his mission. The therapist may assist by asking clarifying questions:

Alan Jenkins

> *What will it mean to you/say about you if you can really face your*
> *abuse and feel about what you have put (the victim) through?*
> *What would it say about you if you copped out and left (the*
> *victim) to feel and deal with all the pain of your abuse?*
> *Who would be taking responsibility if you copped out?*
> *Would you be prepared to keep yourself in the dark and leave it up*
> *to (the victim) to sort out the mess?*

---------- Secondly, the man may be warned about the difficulty of this
task and invited to evaluate his readiness
to commence it:

> *If you really let yourself feel about what you did to (the victim)*
> *and really face your own shame, you will at first feel much worse*
> *than you ever have before. Can you handle such a task?*

---------- Thirdly, he may be reminded of steps he has already taken
which demonstrate some understanding of the impact of the
abuse. The therapist regularly will need to help the man to
recognize and label his achievements, notice the development of
his integrity and inner strength and attribute significance to
these, in the light of his goals. Otherwise, he may become
preoccupied with despair and defeat and lose sight of his gains
in responsibility.

It is helpful for the therapist to anticipate and confirm that the
man will never understand exactly what others are feeling and thinking.
He may wish to enquire of or interrogate the child, in an attempt to try to
understand his/her experience. This exact knowledge of the child's
experience is not important. What is important is his concern about the
impact of his actions and his interest in and commitment to try to
understand what it would be like to be in the childs' position. The child
may not want the man to "know" his/her actual feelings and experience.
Attempts by the man to discuss the impact with the child may be
experienced as intrusive and unwanted if he has not struggled with this
task himself:

I understand that you want to be a more sensitive, understanding and caring
man and that you are hoping that (the victim) will see this in you.

You will need to consider carefully how you proceed. You didn't think of (the
victim's) feelings and what it could mean to the victim at the time. It is now
your job to try to do this thinking - to try to do what you should have done
before - to try to put yourself in (the victim's) shoes.

If you tried to get (the victim) to do this work for you what would this say about you? - what message would it give to (the victim)?

The man may be offered similar invitations to try to understand that impact of his abuse upon his partner and other family members.

This task is facilitated by some of the steps the man has already taken; in particular, facing up to the details of his abuse and accepting responsibility for the abuse. The therapist can also ask specific questions which invite the man to "put himself in the child's and other family member's shoes". Examples of these questions are detailed in Appendix III. I encourage men to study written and videotaped accounts in which victims of sexual abuse describe their experiences. The man is invited to attend to and discuss his emotional reactions to these accounts in order to promote a more "other-centered" or sensitive pattern of remorse. The therapist may prescribe written or taped exercises which require the man to tell the story of the abuse as if he were the child describing exactly what happened and what he was thinking and feeling. Story writing exercises are also prescribed in which the man is required to try to imagine that he is the child at a later stage in his/her life, looking back on the abuse and describing obstacles and difficulties that s/he is facing as a consequence.

IMPLEMENTING THE MISSION PART 2
-CONTEXTUALIZING THE ABUSE

In part 1 of the mission, the process of engagement is applied to facing up to the abuse. Restraints to the man acknowledging, accepting responsibility for and understanding the impact of the abuse are externalized and the man is invited to challenge these restraints.

In part 2 of the mission, the process of engagement is applied to the task of locating the abuse within the wider context of the man's patterns of avoidance of responsibility and reliance on others in family, marital and other relationships. The man is invited to develop explanations for his abuse which address the inevitable preoccupation, "Why the abuse occurred?" from the perspective of the theory of restraint. In this way, a broader range of restraints to responsibility can be externalized and challenged.

I have already discussed the fact that most sexual offenders are puzzled about the reasons for their abuse. Their own theories and explanations are generally unhelpful and restraining, in that they promote avoidance of responsibility for the abuse. Part 2 of the mission aims to develop explanations which promote the man facing pressures and accepting responsibilities extending beyond those related to the specific incidents of abuse. Explanations should help the man to engage in more responsible behaviour and become less reliant on others, in all aspects of his relationships. Explanations should also assist others in the man's family to take less responsibility for the man's behaviour and to decline his "invitations" to face his pressures and responsibilities for him. Helpful explanations promote self-responsibility rather than self-denigration and address restraints at all levels of context. They point to a direction for experimenting in new behaviour for the man and for other family members.   I prefer to focus on restraints which are current in the man's life and seek a variety of ways to put the following questions to him:
What has stopped you from taking responsibility to develop respectful and sensitive relationships with (the victim)/others?

What has stopped you from facing your responsibilities as a father/husband etc?

What has stopped you from taking responsibility for your abuse of (the victim)?

I find it helpful to commence this process by declining the man's invitation to consider "Why?" and inviting him to instead discuss "How?" he has established a pattern of abuse and "How?" he has been training himself in abusive and exploitative practices. This is an extension of the work on facing up to details of the abuse, with a specific focus on antecedents to abusive acts such as patterns of thinking and fantasy associated with the abuse, the planning of abusive acts, the choice of victims and justifications for and ways of maintaining abusive behaviour. Examples of questions designed to elicit such information are presented in Appendix III.

In this way, many of the man's restraining ideas and patterns of thinking which are associated with avoidance of responsibility, can be identified and externalized. Restraints may initially be considered at the individual level of context. The man can then be invited to consider his patterns of avoidance of responsibility within an interactional context - how they are maintained through patterns of reliance on the child, his partner, other family members and other significant persons, to face and carry his responsibilities for him. Patterns of reliance are conceptualized as restraints at the interactional level of context.

These patterns of avoidance and reliance can be further considered within the developmental level of context, in terms of habits and practices which the man has practiced, rehearsed and "trained-in" throughout his life. Finally, these patterns can be considered within the socio-cultural context in terms of their fit with cultural myths and traditions. The man is invited to identify and challenge restraints at all levels of context. A summary of restraints which may be active at different levels of context is presented in Appendix V.

THE CONTEXT FOR PARENTAL INCOMPETENCE

Whilst helping the man to examine the way in which he set up a pattern of abuse with the victim, the therapist may invite him to consider the abuse within a **broader context of parental incompetence**. He will already have considered ways in which he deceived and exploited the child and ways in which he set up the child to carry responsibility for his sexually abusive actions. In broadening the context, he may be advised that "abuse never occurs in a vacuum" and encouraged to consider other ways in which he avoided or failed to face the responsibilities of a parent/uncle etc. and ways in which he relied on his partner or the child to carry his responsibilities for him. The therapist may proceed to enquire:

What kind of parental responsibilities did you face or handle well?

What kind of parental responsibilities did you avoid or leave up to your partner?

What things did you do for the kids?

What things did your partner do for the kids?

- Who put the most effort into the kids growing up?

- Who did the kids approach when they needed help?

- How did you respond when the kids had problems or needed attention?

I find it helpful to invite the man to discuss the **history of his relationship with the child** and the way in which he shaped this relationship over time.

The man may discuss initial difficulties in handling or relating to the child, especially if he was an inexperienced step-parent entering an established family. Feelings of jealousy regarding the child's relationship with his partner and insecurity about his own lack of influence on the child and his inability to establish a close relationship with the child, may have troubled him. He may have showed little sensitivity to the child's feelings about him joining the family and behaved in an angry, resentful or rejecting manner. I find it helpful to invite the man to speculate about the child's experience and feelings and about the responsibility he feels he should have taken in these circumstances:

What did you find difficult to handle at that time?

What do you think (the victim) found difficult to handle at that time?

How did you handle these problems?

How did you respond to (the victim)?

What do you think a parent's responsibility is, in this situation?

How would have liked to have handled it back then?

An abusive man will often have totally unrealistic expectations which are entirely inappropriate, given the child's age. He may describe overly strict and rigid ideals and behaviour which is exploitative, abusive and neglectful. Sexual abuse may be the only form of "closeness" he established with the child. Once again, he is invited to speculate about the child's experience and his responsibility, in this context. The following extract was written by a man who sexually abused his five year old stepdaughter:

My sexual abuse of "Susan" was however, not the only abuse which I inflicted upon her. In the most profound sense I had abused "Susan" by my hardness towards her. I had smacked her. I had yelled at her. I had refused to cuddle her. I had failed to understand the trauma that she suffered after her family and (father) had been wrested from her and in my strict demand for obedience, I had caused her anguish and frustration at not being able to fully please me. The sexual mistreatment was a continuation of all that had proceeded by way of physical, mental and spiritual abuse.

In the past I had failed to have "Susan" love me and to feel close to her. Where I couldn't force her physically to respond to me nor mentally to show a positive attitude towards me, I was able to control "Susan" and get her to be close through sexual means.

Inappropriate boundaries may have been established with the child and other family members, other than sexual abuse. The man's behaviour may have been overly intrusive and the child's privacy and rights may not have been considered. Adult and child business are often mixed up in a variety of ways. An alliance with the child may have been established from which his partner and other family members were excluded. The man is invited to consider how he shaped this alliance - how he invited the child onto the "adult platform", gave privileges or encouraged the child to be critical of and competitive with his partner. In these circumstances, he is once again invited to speculate about the child's and his partner's experience and consider his responsibility.

If the man pursued his own ideas and whims and left most responsibility for the childrens' welfare to his partner, he is invited to consider his partner's experience and his responsibility in this context.

Some abusive men regard themselves as very competent and caring parents. They see themselves as very close to their children, interested and involved in their children's welfare and sensitive and empathic regarding their children's feelings and needs. Often they are extremely popular with children.

Some of these men have difficulties with and tend to avoid close and intimate relationships with adults and seem to invest mostly in relationships with children. Others, however, maintain close and intimate relationships with adults as well as their investments in children. Most take offense at being accused of avoiding or failing to meet their responsibilities as parents.

The therapist may invite such a man to examine his own parenting and attend to gaps and lapses in his sensitivity to the child's feelings and needs and in facing parental responsibilities:

Given your high level of caring and understanding of (the victim's) feelings, how were you able to neglect his/her needs and take advantage of him/her with your abuse?

How did you fail to realise (the victim's) distress and desire for the abuse to stop?

Were you helping (the victim), or helping yourself?

How did you manage to pull the wool over your eyes and convince yourself that you were doing (the victim) no harm?

How were you able to convince yourself that you were still sensitive to (the victim's) feelings and putting his/her needs first when in fact you were using him/her?

When was the first time you noticed there were gaps in your sensitivity to (the victim's) feelings and needs and in your handling of the responsibilities of a parent?

Such questioning and discussion invites the man to examine responsibilities he has avoided or neglected and to consider the significance of his excessive reliance on his partner and the child to face and bear his responsibilities for him. He may then be able to recognize that he was able to continue to avoid responsibility by taking advantage of his partner's and the child's loyalty and support and by using them to protect him from the normal pressures of parenting and the consequences of his actions:

In what ways did you lean on Jill/(the victim) to face your pressures and your responsibilities for you?

How long have you been leaning on Jill/(the victim)?

How long have you relied on Jill/(the victim) to prop you up/carry your problems and responsibilities for you?

What effect has this had on Jill/(the victim's) life over time?

What effect has this had on your life over time?

What steps have you taken since then to stand on your own two feet/to help them throw off these responsibilities?

How did you pull the wool over your own eyes so that you were able to think that you were actually doing your job and even helping them, when in actual fact you were using them?

What would have happened if (the victim) had not told of the abuse?

What would have happened if you had continued to rely on/be propped up by Jill/(the victim)?

What would it have meant for your future?

What would it have meant for Jill's/(the victim's) future?

In this way, the man can also be invited to examine time-trends and the relative influence of patterns of reliance in his own life and in the lives of family members.

Patterns of avoidance of responsibility and reliance on others may be further externalized when examined within a developmental context. The man may be invited to speculate about the extent to which he has been "sucked in" by family traditions of avoidance and reliance and the extent to which he is "following in the footsteps" of certain family members.

THE CONTEXT FOR SOCIAL-EMOTIONAL "IMMATURITY"

Whilst examining the way in which the man set up his pattern of abuse, patterns of self-centered thinking and insensitivity to the needs and feelings of others will be evident. He may be invited to examine his **social-emotional or "immaturity"** within a broader context. He will already have begun to realize the extent of his insensitivity to the child's and to his partner's needs, regarding his abuse, in Part 1 of his mission. Insensitive and self-centered thinking and behaviour are also likely to be evident in other aspects of his relationships. Patterns of **reliance on the child** to attend to man's pressures and responsibilities can be externalized:

In what ways, apart from your abuse, did you neglect or overlook (the victim's) needs and feelings?

Looking back on your contact with (the victim)/other children, do you think you had your needs or their needs mostly in mind?

Whose needs did you let come first?

Do you think you were helping (the victim) to grow up or using (the victim) for your own purposes?

Do you think you were looking after (the victim's) feelings and needs or trying to get (the victim) to look after your feelings and needs?

Do you think you were able to see (the victim) the way s/he really was or only the way you wanted him/her to be?

What sort of needs were you trying to satisfy in yourself by ripping off (the victim)?

How was leaning on (the victim)/using (the victim) as a prop, affecting his/her life?

How was this affecting your life?

What would have happened if you had continued in this way?

The context can be broadened further if the man examines his insensitivity and avoidance of responsibility within the **marital context**:

Who has thought most about/been most concerned about/been most understanding of, others' feelings in the family?

Who shows most sensitivity/understanding/patience?

Who has put most effort into your marriage?

Who has worked hardest for togetherness?

Who has taken most responsibility for remembering/ organizing/planning etc. in your marriage?

Patterns of **imbalance in responsibility and hierarchy/status** may be externalized when the therapist enquires about each partner's way of dealing with pressures, problems and conflict in the marriage:

How have you/how has Jill handled pressures and problems in your marriage and family?

Who is most likely to try and face a problem/try to sort it out/try to do something about it?

When the going gets tough/when the pressure is on, which of you is most likely to:

- *try to lay down the law?*
- *crack up/use violence?*
- *get drunk?*
- *withdraw/go out/try not to think about it/sulk?*
- *blame someone else/criticize?*
- *take it out on someone else?*

The man is invited to examine time-trends in the relative influence of these patterns of imbalance and reliance and to speculate about the consequences for both himself and his partner, if these patterns were to continue.

Patterns of reliance can be further examined in the broader developmental and socio-cultural contexts, particularly as they relate to imbalances in hierarchy/status and social-emotional responsibility between men and women. The therapist may enquire about the extent to which the man has been "sucked in" by traditional blueprints for relating and problem solving and the extent to which he has been making his own decisions about these matters.

THE CONTEXT FOR "SELF-ESTEEM"

Whilst examining the way in which the man has set up his pattern of abuse, restraining patterns of thinking which tend to be associated with "**poor self-esteem**", may become evident. The man is likely to be preoccupied with a sense of inadequacy and insufficiency which may be pervasive in much of his experience. Many men reveal, in their explanations of abusive actions, an unfulfilled but desperate desire for status, approval and to be held in high esteem by others. It is evident that these men struggle unsuccessfully to find acceptable and satisfying ways of meeting these needs.

This thinking becomes evident when the therapist asks questions like the following:
What led you to choose (the victim) as a target for your abuse?
What attracted you to (the victim)?
The man may respond with explanations such as:
She was my little girl - my little parcel of joy.
She seemed so little and beautiful.
I used to look forward to showing her and giving her pleasure.
She was my precious little thing.
He was so cuddly - he liked it so much
He looked up to me and wanted to be with me
She was just there - she was so loving and affectionate.
In these explanations, the child is referred to as available, vulnerable, small, innocent, naive and compliant. It is evident that these qualities are attractive to many offenders. Some men fulfil a fantasy in which they achieve temporary feelings of status and importance along with an "adolescent" thrill of conquest, when they abuse. Others merely describe child victims as easy, available and accessible. There is no doubt that it is easy to trick a child into sexual abuse. It is easy to use a child as a kind of "status object", given that the child is not able to successfully challenge or make demands of the man and is likely to conform to his wishes and directions. This provides an easy way for some men to feel that

Alan Jenkins

they are strong and powerful providers with adoring "partners" who are willing to learn from them. Adult relationships are challenging because adults generally expect to be treated as equal partners to have their needs considered. Adult relationships require some interpersonal skill. It is easy to dominate, to have influence over, to have one's own way with and to "own" a child.

The man who has sexually abused a child can be invited to consider ways in which he has avoided normal pressures and demands associated with relating to adults and adult life:

What is the difference between the way you set up your sexual abuse of (the victim) and the way you would set up a sexual relationship with an adult?

Why do you think you chose to abuse (the victim) rather than set up a sexual relationship with an adult?

If the man describes dissatisfactions in his marriage or work relationships, as antecedents to his abusive behaviour, he may be invited to consider how he has responded to pressures and problems in these relationships and the responsibility he has taken to attend to these difficulties:

How did you handle these pressures/problems?

In what ways did you face them and in what ways did you cop out from them/take them out on others/look for the easy options?

What responsibility would you like to have taken?

The therapist may assist the man to externalize a pattern of reliance on the child to meet his needs for "self-esteem" and to examine time trends in the relative influence of this pattern:

Do you think that you were trying to help (the victim) to feel OK or do you think you were using him/her to try and make yourself feel OK?

Do you think you were supporting (the victim) or do you think you were training (the victim) to support you?

How much did you face problems and pressures in your marriage/work etc. and how much did you cop out into a fantasy world in which you used (the victim) to prop you up?

How much did you face your own problems and pressures and how much did you dump them on (the victim) to carry for you?

What effect has this had on (the victim)?

What effect has it had on you and your ability to cope with life/feel confident in yourself?

What would have happened if you had continued in this way?

What would it mean if you continued to take the easiest option?

The therapist may also invite the man to consider and examine similar patterns of reliance on his partner's submissions and deference, for a sense of status and approval.

This pattern of reliance which relates to the man's desire for status and approval, is illustrated in the following extract from a letter which was written by a man to his two stepdaughters, whom he abused:

I believe I behaved atrociously towards you. I don't just mean the sexual abuse either. That was only one aspect of being a terrible parent. I tried to control your lives totally by being critical of your friends and expecting you to do what I wanted, when I wanted and how I wanted it done. I tried to make you dependent on me. Dependence gives control. For example; while you were doing your homework and I was giving you the answers, it made me feel important and needed, but I gave no thought to you and your needs. I pretended to myself that I was helping you, but in reality I was only helping myself. This was totally selfish. It would have been better for you if I showed you how to find the answers yourself. Another example is when a decision had to be made. When "Kelley" wanted to get a job, I thought it would be too much for her while she was studying. I wanted to control the situation and prevent "Kelley" from making what I saw as a mistake. It is better to let you make your own decisions and learn decision-making for yourself. It was my arrogance that made me think I was right all the time. I gave you no credit for being able to think for yourselves.

I want to tell you the reasons that I wanted to be dependent on you, needed and in control. These in no way excuse what I did. I did not realize these things at the time but that is no excuse either.

One of the reasons was that I felt insecure and afraid of the way people might think of me. I also didn't like myself very much. Having each of you, including your mum, dependent on me made me feel good because I was in control. Not being in control of people scared me. So I pretended to myself that I was helping you, but in reality I was depending on each of you to help me overcome that fear. It is my responsibility to deal with my fear and lack of self-confidence. I was placing that responsibility on you. It is unfair for anyone to place that responsibility on others and it was cruel and gutless of me to place it on you as children. I tried to opt out.

The sexual abuse was part of this. I thought that if I could make you feel special by physically exciting you, then I could make you like me. I wanted to be in control of your feelings towards me. I needed to have your approval of me. To do this I used you without giving any thought to what you needed or thought. I gave no regard to your rights as human beings and in fact I used you as though you were just objects and not people at all. This saddens and disgusts me. I don't know how you managed to put up with my dreadful attitude and repulsive actions for so long.

These patterns of reliance may also be considered within broader developmental and socio-cultural contexts, particularly with respect to the influence of traditions of sexual conquest and status as criteria for male self-esteem and developmental experiences which led to "training" in social-emotional avoidance.

THE CONTEXT FOR SEXUAL PRE-OCCUPATION

An examination of the way in which the man set up his pattern of abuse is likely to reveal patterns of **sexual preoccupation**, particularly when considering the man's emotional state and experience prior to abusive incidents. Many abusive men tend to "think" with their penises rather than their heads and "sexualize" many of their day to day needs and feelings. This becomes particularly apparent in the explanations of some men:

I was only trying to show love to her.
I loved her too much.

These men learn to attribute sexual meaning to their feelings and needs for closeness, affirmation and approval and consequently, they look for sexual solutions to problems, in this context. The man may feel lonely, insufficient or anxious and try to meet his needs with sexual behaviour, generally by engaging in very frequent sexual activity which requires little interpersonal skill. Masturbation, child sexual abuse and paraphilias such as genital exposure and voyeurism are all examples of sexual activity which can be used for this purpose.

The man's explanations may reveal self-centered, "adolescent" preoccupations with sexual conquest and romance:

We were like boyfriend and girlfriend - we were in love - we wouldn't think of anything else.
I used to think about us going away together or getting married.

In these scenarios the man has imagines himself as a young suitor and has abdicated his adult or parental role.

The man is invited to broaden the context and examine his failure to face responsibility for attending to his own needs and feelings

Invitations to Responsibility

and his pattern of reliance on the child to meet these needs. He may also have relied on his partner's support and tolerance of sexual behaviour and interests which she found disagreeable or exploitative. Time trends in the relative influence of these patterns of reliance and the man's responsibility are then considered, in this context.

Some men may also establish patterns of reliance on their victim's which enable then to avoid facing their own sexual fears and self-doubts. A man who sexually abused his eight year old stepdaughter, describes such a pattern in the following extracts from a written, facing up exercise:

I find myself very concerned whilst making love that (partner) enjoys herself. The goal being to bring (partner) to a climax. This is very important to me and if I can't accomplish this then I feel as though I have failed. With "Leanne" there was never any worry about failing with her. She always seemed to enjoy what I did and I didn't have to live up to any standard or try to be the best bed partner. With "Leanne" things were so simple. The simplest of things seem to give her so much pleasure.

The other problem I have is my penis. My penis is a lot smaller than the average size and I have known this for years. I can recall my mum and dad remarking about its size when I was very young but in a joking manner. At some stage I became very self-conscious about this problem, particularly when I was in scouts. We would shower together on camp weekends and I can remember I would go to the toilet and play with my penis, not masturbate as such, but pull on it to make it partially erect. Then I could go to the showers without fear of being made fun off. I can recall one weekend at camp when everyone was hit with the toothpaste trick around their genital areas. Come my turn to wear it, it took the whole tent of kids to hold me down. I of course became a laughing stock because of the small size of my penis.

As I grew, this problem stayed with me. Even when I was married I couldn't let (partner) see my penis at its normal size. Even in the Army I had to play with my penis before I could shower with the fellows.

With "Leanne" I didn't have to worry about any of this. To see her enjoy the stimulation was more than enough for me. I was amazed by her ability to enjoy what I did to her. Her innocence and the fact she was not holding back. "Leanne" even seemed to be able to climax which for me was absolutely the best.

Alan Jenkins

It is often helpful to examine these patterns of sexual preoccupation and reliance on others, within the broader developmental and socio-cultural contexts. Men who have been victims of sexual exploitation and abuse, who have grown up in abusive environments or who have a long history of sexual offending, can be invited to consider the degree of influence of family traditions and other developmental experiences on their current thinking and behaviour:

In what ways do you feel pushed around by your memories of the guy who abused you when you were X years old?

In what ways are those memories still influencing your sexual interests, preoccupations and ideas?

When have you been able to stand up to these preoccupations and ideas?

Are you feeling more or less pushed around by these ideas and preoccupations over time?

It is also helpful to examine these restraints in the light of socio-cultural myths regarding male sexuality and notions of performance, conquest and recipes for intimacy.

THE CONTEXT FOR MISGUIDED ATTEMPTS TO DEAL WITH THE ABUSE

Whilst examining the way in which the man has set up his pattern of abuse, he may be invited to consider his own well-intentioned by **misguided and unhelpful attempts** to deal with his abusive behaviour.

The pattern of abusive behaviour often reveals a cycle of self-intoxicating thinking and preoccupation which is punctuated by abusive incidents. The man may be invited to consider ways in which he has avoided attending to and addressing this cycle, by distracting himself and attempting to justify his abusive behaviour. He can then be invited to consider the extent of his reliance on others, especially the child, to attend to and address his abusive actions for him. In this way, he is invited to take on this responsibility himself and study his own cycle of self-intoxication and abusive behaviour. This process is detailed in Part 4 of the mission - Preventing Relapse:

Who has studied/worried about/thought about your abuse the most?

Who has worked hardest at watching out for/trying to avoid/trying to prevent the abuse?

Who has taken most action to stop the abuse?

What has this meant for you and the amount of responsibility you have accepted, in the past?
What has this meant for (the victim's) life?

The man may also be invited to consider ways in which he has inadvertently maintained a propensity for abuse and exploitation by attending to his established habits of acting on exploitative sexual urges which include:

---------- planning abusive behaviour.
---------- looking for opportunities to "perve" at children.
---------- masturbation to exploitative patterns of thinking and fantasy.
---------- use of exploitative pornography.

He is invited to consider the implications of continuing to act upon these urges and interests in such ways, in the light of his mission and his goals.

IMPLEMENTING THE MISSION PART 3 - DEMONSTRATING RESPONSIBILITY

Having externalized restraints to responsibility within broader contexts, the man is invited to challenge these restraints and demonstrate responsible behaviour both to himself and to others who have been influenced by the abuse. The process of identifying and highlighting patterns of avoidance and reliance often provides sufficient invitation for the man to begin to face new pressures and and practice responsible actions. However, the therapist may facilitate this part of the mission by delivering "irresistible" invitations to responsibility and inviting the man to consider his readiness to plan and engage in new actions. Naturally, the therapist plays an active role in helping the man to discover and appreciate his capacity for responsible and sensitive behaviour, by selecting out and responding to examples of such thinking and behaviour.

The therapist can assist the man in demonstrating responsibility, by inviting him to:

---------- Challenge patterns of avoidance of responsibility and reliance on others and demonstrate:

- **self-responsibility** by attending to his own needs and facing his own pressures;
- **other-responsibility** by developing sensitivity to others needs and feelings;
- **responsibility for facing the consequences of his abuse.**

---------- Establish appropriate and respectful boundaries with the child, his partner and others influenced by the abuse.

CHALLENGING PATTERNS OF AVOIDANCE OF RESPONSIBILITY AND RELIANCE

Demonstrating Self-Responsibility

The therapist can deliver "irresistible" invitations to the man to attend to his own needs and face his own pressures and responsibilities so that the man puts his own arguments for changing his behaviour.

At first questions may be asked which relate to everyday pressures and responsibilities in the man's life:

Could you handle the stress/discomfort of facing up to pressures and responsibilities in your life or would you be prepared to continue a life of copping out, running away, hiding or trying to drink them away?

Could you handle the stress of facing your own pressures and responsibilities and standing on your own two feet or would you be prepared to continue to lean on others and rely on them to prop you up/face your problems for you/do your work for you/carry your load for you?

Could you handle taking the tough path of facing your own pressures or would you be prepared to opt for the easy way of copping out and leaving it to others to face them?

The man may then be invited to attend to specific pressures and responsibilities in his life, such as:

-        **Social - emotional responsibilities**

Would you prefer to learn to face your own feelings/frustrations/ hurts/disappointments and talk them out or are you prepared to continue to take them out on others?

Would you prefer to face the pressure of making your own decisions/running your own life or are you willing to remain a slave to/be pushed around by, your feelings of hurt and disappointment?

Would you rather talk out your problems or continue to take them out on others?

Are you prepared to face your own feelings of hurt and disappointment or would you rather continue to rely on others to look after them for you?

Are you prepared to face arguments and conflict or would you be prepared to continue to run away from them/crack up when the going gets tough?

-        **Self doubts, preoccupations and habits of avoidance relating to "self esteem"**

Are you prepared to earn genuine self-respect by learning to stand on your own two feet or would you settle for a pretence whereby you lean on and use others to try to make you feel OK?

Are you prepared to support yourself or would you be willing to continue to lean on others to prop you up?

Are you prepared to find your own ways to feel OK or would you be willing to continue to try to feel OK at others' expense?

Alan Jenkins

Are you prepared to face the pressures of living in the real world or would you prefer to continue to hide away in a fantasy world?

Are you prepared to develop a genuine recipe for self-respect or would you be willing to continue to let yourself be sucked in by old-fashioned blueprints about sex and dominance?

- ## Sexual preoccupations

Would you prefer to learn to use your head and make your own decisions or would you be prepared to continue to live your life in tow to your penis?

Would you rather use sex for mutual loving and pleasure with a partner or as an anaesthetic/cure for loneliness, insecurity, frustration, anger etc?

Are you prepared to face the pressure of learning to relate equally to adults or would you be prepared to settle for the easy option of using sex as a substitute for relating?

Do you want to be able to get close to others without having to get sexual?

Are you prepared to face your sexual fears and problems or would you be willing to continue to take them out on others?

If the man argues for increased self-responsibility and independence, he may be invited to consider his readiness to act on these arguments and to plan new action. I place particular emphasis on inviting the man to notice achievements he has already made in this direction and to weigh them up when evaluating his readiness to take new action:

What evidence is there that you are ready to face your own pressures and responsibilities and stand on your own two feet?

What signs of self-reliance/independence/responsibility have you recently noticed?

In what ways are you already beginning to stand on your own two feet?

The man can then be encouraged to examine his recent achievements and attribute meaning and significance to them, in terms of his capacity for change and for responsibility:

How have you done this?

Whose idea was it?

How did you cope with (externalized restraint)?

What does it say about you and your ability to handle responsibility/your inner strength?

What will it mean for you if you continue in this way?

He can then be encouraged to plan specific, new responsible actions:

What steps would you take/what would you be doing differently/what pressures would you be facing, if you took further steps towards standing on your own two feet?

The man who has moved out of the family home but into another situation of reliance, such as his parents' home, may be invited to plan new action:

What responsibilities are you facing for yourself?

What responsibilities and pressures are your parents facing for you/saving you from?

What changes would you need to make in your current living arrangements so that you are standing more on your own two feet?

The man who has moved out but remains excessively reliant on his partner, waiting for her to phone etc., may be invited to consider new activities and establish a wider social network:

What changes would you need to make in your lifestyle so that you are not relying on your partner or family for all your social needs?

What could you do instead of waiting by the phone?

Who else could you talk to?

The tendencies of some men to pursue their partner's will also need to be addressed. This process is illustrated clearly in the section dealing with spouse abuse (see Invite the Man to Consider his Readiness to take New Action - page 91).

When new plans for action are discussed, the therapist may help to externalize restraints or obstacles to them being realised:

What would you be up against?

What could stop you/hold you back?

At all times, the therapist should be vigilant for opportunities to select out and highlight instances of responsible action and self-reliance which are evident in the man's behaviour and descriptions of events. In this way, he can be helped to discover his own capacity for responsible action and to attribute to it significance for his mission and goals.

Demonstrating Other-Responsibility

The therapist may invite the man to further develop his sensitivity to other's needs and feelings. He will already have commenced his task in relation to persons influenced by his abuse. In a broader context, however, he can be invited to consider others' feelings about the way he has related to them as a partner/parent etc. and the wider responsibilities he has avoided. Exercises that he has written using his understanding of others' perspectives, as detailed in Part I of the mission - "Understanding the Impact", can be amended to include these new realizations. He can also be invited to extend his developing sensitivity to the needs and feelings of others at work and in social settings outside of the family.

Time-trends in his levels of sensitivity and "other- responsibility" can be considered:

Do you think you are becoming more or less understanding and considerate of others' feelings - in your marriage/family/work?

Are you becoming more of a giver or more of a taker in your marriage/family/work relationships?

What signs/evidence are you seeing that tell you this?

What signs/evidence do you think others would be noticing in you?

In what ways are you filling the voids or gaps of the past in your sensitivity and understanding?

How is this new sensitivity and consideration affecting you and your life?

In what direction do you think you are heading?

Demonstrating Responsibility for the Consequences of the Abuse

The man will have already demonstrated significant responsibility whilst attending to Part 1 of his mission. This process can be extended by inviting the man to consider his readiness to face the full consequences of his abuse.

He may be invited to consider consequences associated with the criminal justice system and determine the way that he plans to demonstrate responsibility in this context. This requires that he assess his readiness to accept that legal proceedings are a consequence of his abusive actions rather than a result of a conspiracy of the system. He can be invited to consider his ability and readiness to maintain his mission of responsibility, within a threatening and somewhat arbitrary criminal justice system:

Do you think you will be able to maintain your mission in the face of the "unfairness" and threat of the court system?

He should consider how he will instruct his solicitor and how he plans to plead, in order to maintain his mission and give clear messages to himself and others that he is taking full responsibility for his abuse. The potential impact of his challenging "errors" in police statements or allowing his solicitor to search for legal loop-holes to discredit the child's evidence, should be considered in relation to his goal of demonstrating responsibility.

Before he faces sentencing, the man may be invited to consider his readiness to accept that a prison sentence is a possible consequence of his actions:

Do you think that you would be able to accept this responsibility or do you think you would be consumed by feelings of resentment at the "unfairness" of the system and proceed to throw in the towel?

If he is able to approach sentencing with an awareness that he may have brought a prison sentence upon himself, the man may be invited to consider what he would need to do in order to survive such a sentence and prevent a loss of responsibility and integrity, whilst living in an environment which does not readily promote responsible behaviour:

Would you be able to maintain your responsibility and integrity or would you become increasingly preoccupied with blame, resentment and feelings of persecution?

What would it mean for your future/for the future of (the victim) and others, if you could maintain your responsibility and integrity in such a challenging system?

What would it mean for you/for (the victim) and others, if you succumbed to feelings of blame, resentment and persecution?

What message would this give (the victim) and others?

How would it affect their feelings of responsibility?

What kind of person would you be when you were released?

In a similar way, the man can be invited to consider his readiness to accept parole or welfare restrictions and family members' rejections or feelings of ambivalence, as consequences of his abusive actions rather than as conspiracies against him.

ESTABLISHING APPROPRIATE AND RESPECTFUL BOUNDARIES

When there is evidence that the man accepts responsibility for his abuse and is demonstrating responsible and respectful behaviour in other aspects of his life, he may be invited to consider ways to demonstrate responsibility to those victimized by his abuse and (if appropriate) to contribute to the establishment of appropriate and respectful boundaries within his family.

Alan Jenkins

When family members do not desire to reunite or re-establish contact with the man, the best way that he can contribute to the establishment of appropriate and respectful boundaries, is to stay away and respect the rights, wishes and privacy of family members.

Whether or not there is a desire to reunite, stay together or re-establish contact, I believe that the man has a duty to try to declare his acceptance of responsibility for the abuse and his understanding of its consequences upon others. This declaration cannot put right what he has done wrong. It may, however, offer some assistance to family members in correctly attributing responsibility for the abuse to the perpetrator. Of course, family members have the right to refuse to receive or to reject this declaration. However, the man's mission requires that he attempts to make it.

If there is a mutual desire for re-unification or re-establishing contact, then the need for the man to take an active role in contributing to the development of appropriate and respectful boundaries between himself and other family members, is paramount, as is the need for him to demonstrate responsibility for his abusive actions.

Establishing Appropriate and Respectful Marital Boundaries

When re-unification is desired, I generally address the man's role, in contributing to respectful and appropriate marital boundaries, within a couple therapy context, before he rejoins his partner. The reasons for working in a couple therapy context are identical to those detailed in the section on couple therapy with spouse abuse (see page 103). As with the spouse abuser, I will generally already have made contact with the partner, following the first or second appointment, in order to ensure that therapy is sensitive to family members' needs and to understand her perspective regarding the abuse as well as her hopes for the future. Some principles for applying the ideas of engagement and responsibility to therapy with the man and his partner are elaborated in this book.

Establishing Respectful and Appropriate Boundaries with the Victim

-   Making a formal apology

An appropriately timed formal apology can be an event in the man's mission which is significant and moving both for himself and family members. It is a step which requires much preparation and planning by the man and one which should be approached cautiously and thoroughly by the therapist.

The man should first be helped to evaluate his readiness to approach this task. He needs to have already put in the ground work, by respecting the child's privacy and space, maintaining distance and not pressuring family members either directly or indirectly, to re-establish contact or to reunite. Convincing evidence must exist that the man has fully acknowledged and accepted full responsibility for his abusive actions. He must have demonstrated more than an intellectual understanding of the potential impact of his abuse.

An apology is a ritual for declaring and demonstrating his acceptance of responsibility which requires an understanding and acceptance of the need to put the child's and other family members' needs first. The apology is regarded as a "gift" of the man's realization of what he has done to the child and his unequivocal acceptance of responsibility for his actions. It should not include any advice for the child or any expectation about how the child should receive it or consequently behave and think. It is given to help lift the burden of responsibility from the child and should contain no requests for or expectations of forgiveness.

If these conditions are not met, then the man is unready to begin the process of making an apology which would then be meaningless and could even be destructive and disrespectful to the child and other family members. If the man regards the apology in a self-centered manner, perhaps as a "ticket home", then he is clearly not ready to make it. This is evident in the statement of one man who exclaimed:
I've said I'm sorry, now why can't I go home?

When the man has met the conditions for readiness, he may begin to prepare himself for the apology. I encourage men to write letters or make tapes of apology, in which they rehearse their message and get feedback from the therapist. Guidelines for the preparation of such letters and tapes of apology are presented in Appendix VI. When the man is satisfied with his letter or tape he may decide to use it as a way of communicating the message of apology or as an initial step before making a "face to face" apology, at a later time. The letter or tape may not be sent at all and may not even be wanted by the child or other family members. However, the task of writing a letter or making a tape still constitutes a useful step for the man in organizing his thinking and attempting to get his message across. His mission requires that he attempt the task and try to declare his responsibility.

This process may culminate in a **"public" apology** especially if there is a mutual desire for reunification of the family or to establish access with the man. I prefer to arrange for a "public" apology to take place in the presence of the child's counsellor and all other family members and significant persons. The "public" apology constitutes a ritual which is "public" in that it takes place in the presence of all significant people influenced by the abuse. This ensures that no vestiges of secrecy remain in the family. It offers an opportunity for the man to declare his realizations and responsibility and for both parents to state clearly and publicly, their commitment to a transition from the "old order" - the way the family was, to a "new order" or new direction for the family. This can provide clarification and reassurance for all family members.

It is evident that the man's apology must extend beyond the abuse itself and refer to all the ways in which he has let family members down or failed to face his responsibilities. He will of course have apologies to make to family members other than the child and to others who have been influenced by the abuse, based on his realizations of what he has put each of them through. The man's partner may also wish to apologize for ways that she feels she has let family members down - for example, failing to believe the child, blaming the child for the abuse etc. However, her responsibilities are kept separate and distinct from the responsibility for the abuse itself which the man takes fully on his own shoulders.

Re-establishing Contact

When family reunion or the establishment of access are mutually desired, the man is helped to evaluate his readiness for such a step. He must accept the need to put the needs of others first and to give due regard to the readiness of all family members. The therapist may invite him to take responsibility to "put the brakes on" and to earn the right to take this step:

Is it still important that you take responsibility to try to earn the respect of family members and proceed at their pace or would you be prepared to try to set your own pace and demand/expect/pressure their respect and acceptance of you?

Given that you betrayed your role, is it important to you that you try to earn back the privilege of living with your family having access with (the victim), or do you regard it as a right which is yours for the taking?

The man is encouraged to be wary of his own and others' tendencies to rush things or try to push the pace. He is invited to question the motives of other family members who try to hurry things along, rather than be "sucked in" by them - particularly in the light of established patterns of others looking after his feelings and carrying his responsibilities for him:

Whose job is it to put the brakes on - the adults or the children's?
Whose job is it to ensure that the kids needs, in the long term, are being fully considered?

Reunification and access generally work best if they are gradually introduced and preceded by "public" meetings of therapists and family members in which previous steps are evaluated and new steps are planned.

Once contact is established between the man and the child, his mission is extended and intensified as he faces the responsibility of **active boundary setting** with the victim. His job is to demonstrate unequivocally clear, appropriate and respectful boundaries in every contact he has with the child. Everything that he does and says will give the child a message either of respect of his/her rights, body, privacy or one of disrespect. This part of the mission is regarded as vital and the man is encouraged to operate on the principle of "overkill", by not missing an opportunity to set appropriate and respectful boundaries:

Are you ready to take every opportunity you can to demonstrate to (the victim) in both words and actions:
- that you respect his/her rights/privacy/body?
- that you understand and respect the difference between a father and a child?
- that there is no way you will violate or betray this responsibility again?

The man is encouraged to look for opportunities and to invent ways to get this message across. This may mean learning to knock on doors before entering rooms, not entering bathrooms when a child is present, learning to understand and set realistic expectations, etc. He is encouraged to anticipate the fact that the child may slip back into some of the old and inappropriate patterns of behaviour that he encouraged, in the past. The child may, for example, appear to invite the man to re-establish

Alan Jenkins

inappropriate alliances which exclude his partner or engage in inappropriate sexual behaviour. He is encouraged to respond to such behaviour, should it arise, in ways which re-enforce clear and appropriate parent-child and husband-wife boundaries. *For example, a man who sexually abused his twelve year old daughter, encouraged her to take on responsibilities more appropriate to his partner. He would discuss major decisions in the family with her and would encourage her to criticize and berate her mother. He engaged in "intimate talks", "like we were boyfriend and girlfriend", with her. His partner felt excluded, that she was "in the way" and tended to withdraw from them both. She felt angry at her daughter's "seductive" and "flirtatious" behaviour with her father and felt that the child could "twist him around her little finger".*

When this family reunited some time later, the man planned ways to avoid inviting his daughter and to refuse any of her attempts to step on the "adult platform" again. He decided to consult with his partner regarding any decisions about their daughter's behaviour and her future and to refuse to act unilaterally. This meant no private talks with the daughter and sharing all information with his partner. His resolve was to act together with his partner as a marriage and parenting team and not to allow their daughter to slip back into old habits and alliances which he had promoted and encouraged in the past.

His partner also planned new ways to establish appropriate mother-daughter boundaries and decided to take a more active role as a mother and involve herself more in her daughter's life and future. This required her to understand how her daughter's behaviour was shaped in the direction of an unhealthy alliance with her father, so that she could stop blaming and competing and begin supporting and helping. Naturally, the woman needed to share responsibility for the establishment of appropriate and healthy boundaries in the family. She was, however, able to distinguish these responsibilities from the responsibility for the abuse which she learned to attribute to her husband.

The man is encouraged to anticipate and understand that family members, especially those most influenced by the abuse, will feel some ambivalence and discomfort about him re-establishing contact. This is regarded as appropriate and healthy because it suggests that family members are not hiding their feelings or engaging in overly protective behaviour towards the man. He is encouraged to avoid the fantasy of being accepted back into the family without any fears and discomfort.

Expressions of anger, fear and ambivalence are to be anticipated and welcomed as indications that family members are working through the impact and consequences of the man's betrayal.

I find it useful to corroborate the man's perceptions of his success in getting his message of responsibility across to family members and in establishing appropriate and respectful boundaries, by making contact with the therapist who works with the child. If the man's message of responsibility is getting through to the child, this will be evident in the child's counselling sessions. When this evidence is not forthcoming, the man is obliged to try to find more active ways to attend to this aspect of his mission. The onus is on the man, at all times, to help the child feel respected and his/her own person.

The man and his partner will eventually need to find ways to share responsibility for parenting, to act as a unit and to find an appropriate mix of support, understanding and corrective discipline for inappropriate behaviour, with the abused child and other children in the family.

IMPLEMENTING THE MISSION PART 4 - PREVENTING RELAPSE

This stage of the mission requires the man to discover effective ways to disrupt established patterns (of exploitative thinking and abusive behaviour) in his offending. It is presented as a final step in the man's mission, in order to emphasize its ongoing relevance even in situations where contact with the child has been re-established. Relapse prevention may, however, be addressed quite early in therapy, particularly if the man feels that he is unable to control his abusive behaviour, there is evidence of multiple victims and offences or if his expectations and goals are extremely unrealistic and appear to be based solely on wishful thinking and hope (for example, men who express a strong denial of the likelihood of recurrence of abuse and denial of any sexual interest in children).

Patterns of offending can be extremely enduring and influential in the man's life, especially when he continues restraining habits and practices by which he distracts himself from and avoids attending to his abusive thoughts and actions. The man's earlier work in facing up, detailing the pattern of offending and contextualizing the abuse will have helped him to challenge these habits and practices of avoidance. However, old practices and habits tend to "re-establish themselves" when the man does not maintain his vigilance. It is essential that he extends this responsibility and develops effective and ongoing ways to attend to and disrupt patterns of offending.

The therapist may spend considerable time in helping the man to appreciate the need for this stage of the mission, particularly if he has successfully attended to responsibilities at other stages.

I generally introduce this stage by asking the question:
How have you dealt with sexual feelings or urges towards (the victim)/children, when they have arisen, in recent times?

The man may exclaim that he is no longer feeling any sexual interest in the child or in other children and has not for a considerable time. I do not find it helpful to challenge the validity of these assertions.

The man may not have noticed any feelings of sexual interest in or desire to exploit children, while working on the early steps of the mission and while facing the challenge of court proceedings. I do, however, attempt to invite the man to consider the meaning of his experience in the context of predictable events in the future and his goal never to re-offend. I find it helpful to express respect for his commitment and resolve never to re-offend and then I attempt to normalize the predictable recurrence of feelings of sexual interest in children:

I respect your commitment to quitting abuse and understand your belief that you will achieve this if you no longer feel any sexual urges towards children. However, old feelings, urges and habits associated with your past sexual abuse of (the victim) are powerful and resilient and will reappear and try to stick their noses into your business again.

I encourage the man to avoid complacency:

Now is not the time to get sucked in to a false sense of security but a time for increased vigilance.

Once again, I predict the inevitable recurrence of urges and suggest a new criterion for the man to evaluate success in his mission:

You will experience sexual feelings or urges again with (the victim) and other children. In fact, I am surprised you haven't already. Frankly, the sooner you do the better. Then you can learn to face them and deal with them in responsible ways. Only then can you feel genuinely confident that you have put abuse behind you. Otherwise your confidence is based more on hope and wishful thinking.

Do you think you could be 100% sure that you will never abuse again without having tested yourself and proved that you can say "No" to any urge, however strong, that might enter your mind?

In this way, the man is invited to seek and welcome evidence of sexual urges and to externalize and challenge restraints which promote avoidance of this responsibility. These restraints generally relate to confusion between urge and action and a fear that any evidence of sexual urges towards children, if acknowledged, will result in abusive actions. Many men try to avoid or suppress such urges, some even going to the extent of trying to avoid contact with children altogether.

I asked one man when he expressed that he had not noticed any sexual urges:

What could be stopping you from noticing them?

He responded:

Alan Jenkins

I don't want to let myself feel those thoughts.

He was then able to detail his fears which were restraining him from noticing and facing his own experience.

The therapist may provide "irresistible" invitations to the man to face his urges and feelings:

Do you want to run your own life or do you want your life to revolve around your urges - with fear of your urges dictating what you should and shouldn't do?

What would it mean if you spent your life on the run/hiding from your urges?

Would you be in charge or would your urges be in charge of you?

Would you be more confident if you knew you could feel an urge but be 100% clear you wouldn't act on it or would you be more confident if you spent your time trying to avoid urges and on the run from your urges?

Under which circumstance would you be more likely to be ambushed by urges in the future?

- *if you practice facing them and saying "No" to them?*
- *if you practice hiding or running from them?*

I explain that many people experience urges to act in inappropriate ways and that the difference between responsible and irresponsible persons is not the experience of urges but the making of responsible decisions about how they will act.

The man is invited to consider his readiness to commence an ongoing process of relapse prevention, in which a lot of hard work lies ahead of him. When he expresses readiness to face this stage, he is invited to attend to his pattern of offending. This requires him to review the development of past incidents of abuse, and pay particular attention to patterns of thinking, feeling and behaviour, how he set up incidents of abusive behaviour, how he shaped the nature of his relationship with the child and patterns of justification and avoidance which helped him to "pull the wool over his eyes". Given that he did not attend to this pattern of offending in the past but left it for others to worry about and take action for him, he is invited to rectify this situation by studying the pattern in detail and identifying warning signals, to which he failed to attend in the past but which could serve as cues to alert him in the future.

Many men who experience their offending as somewhat compulsive in nature, describe cyclical patterns of offending in terms of an escalating experience of self-intoxication in which they become increasingly preoccupied with their own fantasies and feelings of excitement, arousal and urgency at the expense of other rational thoughts. It can be helpful for these men to chart the process of escalating self-intoxication, in the most recent incidents, by recalling patterns of thinking, feeling and behaviour at various points in the cycle. As with spouse abusers, these men can be helped to find an exit point from the cycle which can be readily identified by association with specific cues or warning signals.

The man is encouraged to notice and use these cues or warning signals in current situations, by removing himself from the situation very early in the sequence, before he significantly raises his level of arousal. He may then review his decisions and actions and their consequences, along with future plans, once he has left, rather than engage in an increasingly futile battle with his urges, whilst remaining in the situation.

The following excerpt is from a man's attempt to chart one aspect of his pattern of offending. The man had engaged in a serious of offences which involved him exposing his penis to young children on buses, as well as the sexual assault of his daughter's friend. The following eight steps detail his recollection of his experience of one of these offences. --

---------- *Get onto a bus, walking down the aisle, start checking out the people*

---------- *See a girl (about eleven years old) with long hair, sexy walk*

---------- *Sit as close as possible, preferably opposite*

---------- *Start to check her out whilst pretending to read, thinking "How far is she going - When is she getting off", feeling restless*

---------- *Checking her out more often, thinking "I wonder what she looks like naked", "She wants to see my penis"*

---------- *Feeling excited, eyes transfixed on her, thinking "She wants to see my penis", "No I shouldn't do it", feeling trembly and shaky*

---------- *I can't take my eyes of her, my urges say yes, my mind says no, thinking "I can't control them", "She wants to see my penis", feeling trapped - like in a room with no windows and doors - I can't get out. Trembling and shaking*

---------- *Expose my penis.*

This man was encouraged to chart his recollections of several such incidents and identify warning signals that he could use as cues for new action. He decided to attend to the number of times that he looked at a potential victim. Once he had looked twice at a girl, he would stand up, move to the front of the bus and take a seat facing the driver. If there was no seat he would press the bus stop and stand facing the driver until the bus stopped and then alight. Once seated away from the girl or off the bus, he would then review his actions and the consequences of his behaviour, having left the situation and if he had stayed near the girl.

I occasionally make training audio-tapes which describe successful exits from specific cycles of offending, in order to help the man rehearse this process in imagination before proceeding on to engage in **responsibility testing**. Once he has developed a realistic set of safety procedures, he may be invited to assess his readiness to "face temptation" and go into situations in which he is likely to "trigger" urges and then practice responsible behaviour.

All men are encouraged to be vigilant and to look out for warning signals in their day to day lives. I generally advise them to expect these signals and to welcome them as opportunities to disrupt old patterns, practice responsible behaviour and learn to develop new habits which will eventually replace the old.

The more opportunities the man has to practice disrupting patterns of offending, the weaker these patterns will become as stronger new patterns of responsible behaviour develop.

I often involve partners, at this stage in therapy, in order to help them understand the process of responsibility testing. However, it is the man's responsibility to test himself and not his partners. When warning signals are evident in a family setting, the partner will have important contributions to make in noticing and responding to evidence of the re-emergence of the pattern of re-offending. For example, if there are warning signs of an alliance developing between the child and the man which excludes the woman, both partners are invited to notice and take the opportunity to reaffirm that they are a team and to take action to redefine appropriate boundaries.

The man is encouraged to be especially vigilant and notice even fleeting feelings of sexual interest in the child and other children. When he has such a thought in which he views the child or the child's behaviour in a sexual way, he is advised not to push this thought out of his mind but to take the opportunity to face it and respond in an appropriate and responsible way. This may involve saying "No" to the feeling, leaving the situation and taking time to correct his thinking about the child and the child's behaviour and examine this thinking in an appropriate context. When doing this, the man may review the consequences of acting and not acting on the urge and consider the differences between the kind of man that he was and the kind of man that he is becoming.

The therapist should provide considerable support and permission, in therapy, for the man to talk about his responsibility testing. He will initially demonstrate some reluctance to do so. He can, however, be invited to consider facing responsibility in this way, as an indication of strength rather than weakness and as a further opportunity to link the experience of sexual urges with responsible behaviour.

The man is also invited to challenge any inadvertent maintenance practices which involve ways of acting irresponsibly upon sexual urges towards children. He is encouraged to be vigilant and to notice any tendency to seek or plan opportunities to look at or regard children in sexual ways. This includes patterns of masturbation to fantasies about children. These practices are regarded as ways of acting upon sexual urges which strengthen old patterns of offending. The therapist should take care to help the man discriminate between his experience of an urge and the behaviour of acting upon this urge. He is encouraged to modify his behaviour and thinking in response to urges rather than attempt to modify the urges themselves. The latter is inevitably a futile task which results only in avoidance and distraction; strategies which are restraining to responsibility and which serve to increase the risk of reoffending.

Towards the end of therapy, I may encourage the man to prepare and document a **declaration or letter of "resignation"** from his previously abusive lifestyle. This requires the man to review his goals and achievements and provide evidence to support or "publicly" justify his conviction that he will no longer abuse. A resignation is a formal document which should summarize his understanding of his abuse and what stopped him from accepting responsibility in the past as well as his "qualifications" for moving on to a new lifestyle. These "qualifications" should relate to all aspects of his mission and be convincing to the therapist, his partner and (if appropriate) others influenced by the abuse. The letter of "resignation" should state clearly and unequivocally the kind of person and lifestyle that he is leaving behind and the kind of person that he is becoming and lifestyle that he attends to pursue.

Alan Jenkins

COUPLE THERAPY

In couple therapy, the therapist not only assists the man to demonstrate responsibility to his partner but helps both partners to challenge patterns of interaction which restrain their ability to relate to each other as independent adults. This process is usually extremely challenging for the woman as well as the man. She is likely to face the full impact of her partner's betrayal, her own self doubts and her grief for her own and her childrens' losses and hurts. These are experiences which may have been avoided or denied to some extent, prior to couple therapy.

It is important to note that the aims and consequences of couple therapy are not necessarily reunion. If both partners are less restrained and more able to relate to each other as independent adults, they may not choose to continue a relationship. The woman may acknowledge more fully the depth of her feelings of hurt and betrayal, may feel less obligation or duty to continue an unwanted marriage, may realize she no longer loves or respects the man, may realize that she can cope without him or may decide that she does not want the relationship. Occasionally, the man may decide to terminate the relationship.

The process of couple therapy is similar to that outlined for the spouse abuser and his partner, however, I will describe some specific emphases which relate to sexual abuse.

Initially, I invite both partners to describe, in each other's presence, the impact of the abuse upon their lives and their hopes and goals for the future:

Where has the abuse left you both now?

What has it meant to each of you?

How has it affected your plans and hopes for the future?

What do each of you think needs to happen now?

What changes need to take place in your marriage and family?

What has happened so far?

What changes have each of you noticed?

When asking the last question, I often ask the man:

What changes do you think Jill will have noticed in you ?

In this way, the man is invited to speculate about the impact of attempts he has already made to demonstrate responsibility to his partner. The woman is then invited to comment on the accuracy of his speculations.

The therapist can assist this process by helping to externalize restraints to each partner's **openness** in discussing their feelings and needs regarding the man's abuse and its consequences. This may challenge the oppressive secrecy that is pervasive with sexual abuse:

What things do you think need to be talked about together regarding the abuse?

What have you already talked about?

The man may be asked:

What things do you want Jill to know?

What do you think Jill wants/needs to know?

Do you think Jill can handle/is ready, to hear these things?

What do you think would happen if you told Jill exactly what you did to (the victim)?

Are you ready to take the risk in talking to Jill?

What would happen if you never found the courage to talk to Jill?

The woman may be asked:

What things do you need to know from Jack?

What would it mean to you if Jack told you exactly what he did to (the victim)?

What would it mean to you if Jack told you what he has realized about what he did?"

Do you think he could handle talking to you about this?

Are you ready to take the risk in talking to Jack?

What would happen if you never talked about these things?

The process of having each partner comment on the other's experience not only encourages a tendency to check out each other's experiences but invites each partner to challenge their **own** restraints and make their **own** arguments for openness.

In this way, restraints to openness can be discussed and challenged and both partners are invited to put arguments for more honest and open communication of their feelings and needs, regarding the abuse.

Alan Jenkins

If both partners express a desire to talk more openly about the abuse, they may be warned about the challenges and risks which are inherent in this goal and invited to consider their readiness to share their experiences:

Are you both ready to share your shame and your grief with each other?

The woman may be asked questions like those which follow, after which the man is encouraged to respond to her answers:

Do you think Jack could handle it if you let him know the full extent of how hurt and betrayed you feel - especially on your down days?

Do you think he could understand and handle you feeling untrusting and unforgiving over a long period of time?

Do you think Jack is ready to share his facing up and his shame with you?

Do you think he could handle the pain of facing his shame publicly?

Do you think Jack could handle it if (the victim) let him know the full extent of how s/he feels about the abuse?

The man may be invited to speculate in front of his partner about the extent to which he thinks he has demonstrated responsibility in facing up to his abuse:

What do you think Jill understands about how much you have faced up to and what you have realised about your abuse, so far?

How convinced do you think Jill is that you are taking full responsibility for the abuse?

In this way, the man can receive feedback from his partner about his effectiveness in demonstrating responsibility to her. This may be helpful in inviting him to take a more active role in demonstrating responsibility.

In a similar way, the man may be helped to understand the extent to which his sensitivity and understanding are evident to his partner, and invited to share more of his realizations if the woman is asked questions like the following:

What do you think Jack understands about what the abuse has meant to you and what he has put you through?

Do you think Jack really wants to know what it has meant to you?

What tells you that?

How do you think that he is trying to understand?

Do you think he could understand and handle the truth about what he has put you through?

The woman may also be asked similar questions about her perception of the man's understanding of the impact of his abuse upon the child.

The man may then be asked the following questions:

Are you ready to share with Jill what you have realized about what you think you have put her through?

Part of the man's mission is to assist his partner in developing an **explanation for the abuse** which allows for appropriate attribution of responsibility to the perpetrator. In this way, he can help his partner to throw off any feelings of responsibility for the abuse that she carries. The therapist should first understand the woman's current explanations and theories and her beliefs about her partner's explanations.

The therapist can first ask the man to speculate about his partner's explanations and attributions of responsibility, regarding the abuse:

What do you think Jill puts the abuse down to?

What does she know about what you have realized about that?

What do you think she might have thought initially?

How do you think her thoughts and feelings about that have changed over time?

Do you think she still hangs on to any feelings of responsibility for your abuse?

How have you tried to let her know that you are fully responsible?

The woman is then asked to comment on her partner's perceptions and invited to contrast them with her own opinions:

Is Jack on the right track when he says....?

What do you put the abuse down to?

What do you think Jack puts the abuse down to?

The woman may now be invited to consider the abuse in a broader systemic context:

In what ways was Jack's abuse of (the victim) in character/out of character with the way he handled his responsibilities as a father and as a husband?

In what ways has Jack relied on others to face his pressures and responsibilities for him?

Imbalances in levels of responsibility and attributed status may be externalized and challenged in similar ways to those detailed in couple therapy with the spouse abuser and his partner.

Alan Jenkins

When an **imbalance in responsibility** is acknowledged, the woman may be asked in the presence of her partner:

Do you think Jack wants to take more responsibility as a father/as a husband?

What evidence have you seen of this?

What evidence do you think the children have noticed?

She may then be asked questions like the following:

Do you think Jack wants to take an equal share of responsibility or do you think he wants you to carry some of his load for him?

Other examples of these invitations are detailed in the section on couple therapy with spouses (see page 111).

The man is asked, in the presence of his partner, questions like the following:

Do you think Jill is ready and prepared to share responsibility in your marriage and family?

Further examples of these questions are also presented in the section on couple therapy with spouse abusers.

In a similar way, an **imbalance in attributed status or power** is externalized and challenged. The woman may be asked:

Do you think that Jack is becoming more or less respectful of yours/children's, rights and feelings?

What evidence have you seen of this?

What evidence do you think the children have seen?

Details of invitations for both partners to challenge this pattern of imbalance and develop a more equitable relationship are presented in the section on couple therapy with spouse abusers and their partners (see page 107).

Both partners may be invited to consider ways in which they can **attend to their children's needs and concerns** regarding the abuse.

The man may be invited to consider his responsibilities:

What do you think (the victim) most needs from you now?

What do you want (the victim) to know about what you have realized about your abuse of him/her?

What do you want (the victim) to know about what you have realized about the kind of father you were?

What do you think (the victim) would want to know?

What do you think (the victim's) concerns are/will be in the future?

How can you demonstrate in actions as well as words that you respect (the victim's) rights/privacy/body?

The woman may be invited, in a similar way, to consider her responsibilities:

What do you want (the victim) to know about what you have realized about Jack's abuse of her?

What do you want (the victim) to know about what you have realized about your role as a mother and the relationship you had with her?

What do you think (the victim's) concerns are/will be in the future?

How can you demonstrate to (the victim) that you support, care for his/her feelings and will protect him/her, in future?

In this way, both partners can clarify their very different responsibilities with respect to the abuse, and plan **together** ways in which they can each take responsibility for meeting them.

CONCLUSION

I have found the model of engagement to be particularly helpful for inviting sexual offenders to accept responsibility for and quit their abusive behaviour, and to take responsibility for relating in more sensitive and respectful ways. The model can be applied in individual, couple, family or group therapy settings but has the advantage of requiring that the man's therapy, whatever the format, is sensitive and attuned to the needs and feelings of those influenced by the abuse, particularly family members. The man's mission is, in part, to assist with the resolution of trauma caused by his abuse. This is partially achieved by the man accepting full responsibility and publicly declaring his commitment to this stance. Therapeutic interventions based on this model have a systemic focus and can address restraining patterns of thinking and interaction for both the offender and other family members which prevent appropriate attribution of responsibility to the offender.

The engagement model, while generating strategies and ideas of its own, can offer a template or context in which some of the ideas and strategies employed in other therapy models, can be usefully applied. Even pharmacological approaches which rely on the administration of drugs designed to reduce sexual interest and arousal, could be used in the context of this model, if the man is invited to take responsibility for the management of his medication.

I believe that approaches to therapy with abusive men should be consistent with an ideology of non-violence, respect and cooperation in the wider community. Attempts to address sexual offending, and the context in which it occurs, which are based on the model of engagement are also likely to generate strategies for challenging the continuum of sexual exploitative behaviours in the community and promoting necessary social and cultural changes.

I am wary of attempts to quantify "success" in therapy with sexual offenders. The measurement of detected recidivism is clearly an inadequate criterion. Detected offences represent only a fraction of total offences committed (Russell 1984). I have established a set of criteria to rate attainment of goals which relate to all steps of the offender's mission. I use this admittedly subjective set of criteria to make decisions about when to terminate therapy. I discuss these criteria with the man, his partner and occasionally other family members. When there is sufficient evidence to support significant achievement of goals in all relevant criteria, then therapy is terminated. Follow-up interviews are conducted, when possible, at six month or one year intervals. On average, I would maintain contact with a man, who appears to have fully acknowledged his abuse, over a three year period, although the main bulk of therapeutic work is done in the first six months to one year. It is my impression that goal attainment on all relevant criteria correlates highly with the absence of evidence or allegations of re-offending. This supposition, however, awaits formal research.

In recent years, I have applied the model of engagement to adolescent sexual offenders and their caregivers, particularly after discovering that many adult offenders began "careers" in sexual abuse in early adolescence (Groth et al 1982; Abel et al 1983). There are a number of significant differences in emphasis when working with adolescents. The societal and family contexts for the abuse are different for adolescents and adults. The criminal justice system is clearly more tolerant and less punitive with adolescent offenders. In many cases, the sexual offences of adolescents are regarded as trivial, transient and requiring little intervention (Knopp 1982). Adolescents must accept full responsibility for their abusive actions. Adolescents, however, do not have full adult rights and are not regarded as fully responsible for their own welfare. Their caregivers have a responsibility to establish a family environment which promotes the development of responsible and sensitive behaviour in children. Caregivers of adolescents who abuse are not responsible for the abuse but they do have quite different responsibilities from members of the families of abusive adults. They are expected to help their abusive sons to face responsibility for abuse and relate respectfully to others.

Whilst I use the same principles of engagement when working with adolescents and their caregivers, they are incorporated into a specific model with steps which are quite distinct from the model for working with adults which is detailed in this book. It would be inappropriate and unhelpful to attempt to engage an adolescent offender without also attempting to engage his caregivers.

Alan Jenkins

I generally see the adolescent together with his caregivers at first and attempt to contextualize the abuse with a systemic as well as a developmental context. As with the adult offender, I invite the adolescent to accept responsibility for his abusive behaviour and other aspects of his development and lifestyle. I put equal weight, however, on the engagement of caregivers by inviting them to find effective ways to promote self-responsibility and sensitivity in their adolescent charges.

FACING UP - A MISSION IN RESPONSIBILITY

FACE YOUR ABUSE
Acknowledge the full extent of the abuse;
Face/talk/write about details;
Face embarrassment/shame/fear.

OWN/WEAR YOUR ABUSE
Take full responsibility;
Stop blaming other people/other things;
Stop making excuses;
Understand why it is abuse;
Recognise and own that you have a problem;
Don't make hollow promises.

RESPECT DISTANCE/SPACE FOR THE VICTIM
Deciding to live separately;
Understanding how this can help:
- setting new boundaries;
- communicating responsibility.

UNDERSTAND WHAT YOU HAVE PUT THE VICTIM/OTHERS THROUGH
How it is dangerous and destructive;
How it can affect the victim and others;
Try to put yourself in the victim's shoes.

UNDERSTAND HOW IT HAPPENED/THE DEVELOPMENT OF THE ABUSE
What has stopped you from taking responsibility for relating respectfully and sensitively with others
What has stopped you from taking responsibility for the abuse
How you can quit training as a child abuser.

HELP THE VICTIM TO GET YOUR PROBLEMS OFF HIS/HER BACK
Demonstrating responsibility to the victim and family members;

Alan Jenkins

Distance/space;
Taking full responsibility;
Understanding how it could affect the victim/others.

LEARNING TO RESPECT THE VICTIM (AND OTHERS)
Respecting rights/privacy/others' bodies;
Taking the responsibility of a father/partner etc;
Setting clear boundaries.

FACING THE CONSEQUENCES OF YOUR ABUSIVE BEHAVIOUR
Pressures of legal/welfare system;
Responsibilities to family members.

FACING NEW PRESSURES AND RESPONSIBILITIES
Responsibilities as a parent;
Responsibilities as a partner;
Responsibilities as a family member.

FACILITATING FACING UP   -   ACKNOWLEDGEMENT

AGE OF VICTIM
How old is (the victim)?
How old was (the victim) when you started/ stopped your abuse?

COMMENCEMENT - METHOD OF COERCION
How did you first trick/force/con/bribe (the victim) into sexual abuse?
What did you do to him/her at first? where, when, and how?
What did you get him/her to do to you at first?
What did (the victim) say and do when you first tried to abuse him/her?
What did you say and do then?

ANTECEDENTS
What were the initial danger signs, warnings that you might abuse?
When did you first think about it before this?
What did you think/imagine?
How did you plan it at first - later?
How did you set up opportunities later on?

PROGRESSION OVER TIME
What other things did you do to (the victim) over time?
What other things did you get (the victim) to do to you over time?
How far did you take it?
How far did you want to take it?
How did you trick/force/con/bribe (the victim) into them?
What other ways did you treat (the victim) unfairly?
Who else was involved?

AWARENESS & RESPONSE TO VICTIM'S FEELINGS
When did you first notice that (the victim) was distressed by what you were doing to him/her?
When did you first become aware that (the victim) didn't like what you were doing/wanted you to stop?
When did you first notice (the victim) try to resist/protest/stop it?
- What did s/he do/say?
- What did you do/say then? before that?

Alan Jenkins

What signs did (the victim) show before this that s/he didn't want to do it?

What did you think when you noticed the (victim's) distress/resistance?
- How did you feel?

How did you try to override (the victim's) wishes/feelings?

How did you try to get (the victim) to keep going along with it?

How did you try to keep (the victim's) feelings out of your mind?

How did you try to justify what you were doing, to yourself?

MAINTAINING SECRECY

How did you try to make/get (the victim) to keep it secret?
- bribes/threats/intimidation/requests/guilt-inducement

How did you try to set up opportunities so that no-one would find out?

EFFORTS TO STOP

When did you first try to stop your sexual abuse?

How did you try to stop it?

Did you try to stop it yourself or did you hope that (the victim) would stop it?

How did (the victim) try to get you to stop it?

Who tried hardest to stop it - you or (the victim)?

EXPLANATIONS/JUSTIFICATIONS

How did you try to justify/explain away your abuse:
- at first?
- later on?
- in the face of (the victim's) distress?

(see levels of denial of responsibility - Figure 1)

What was the "good part"/moral side/mature side of you saying about the abuse?

What was the "bad part"/immoral side/immature side of you saying about the abuse?

What stories/pictures did you make up about the abuse to help you to knock out your "good"/moral side?

BREAKING THE SECRET

Who made the first attempt to break the secret?
- What happened?

- What did you do and say to others/to (the victim)?
How was the secret actually broken?
- Who took the initiative?
- Were they believed?
- How did you try to stop people believing (the victim)?
- What happened when you were confronted?
- What did you do/say? How did you feel?
When and how did you admit it?

CONSEQUENCES

How do you feel now that it is out in the open?
How do you feel towards (the victim) now that the secret it out?
How often do you see/spend time with (the victim) now?
How do you treat him/her now?
How do you think (the victim) feels you are treating him/her now?
What have you said to him/her about what you did/about him/her telling?
What have others said/done since it has come out in the open?
What do you think your partner thinks about you?
What does your partner expect of you now?
What would have happened if it hadn't been stopped when it was?
- How far would it have gone
- What would it have meant for (the victim's) future?
- What would it have meant for your future?

OTHER OFFENCES

Who else have you tried to involve in sexual abuse?
Who else have you tried to pick on/harass sexually?
What other kinds of sexual problems have you experienced?
If you hadn't been found out, who do you think would have been next in line?
- What other kinds of sexual problems would you have developed?

Alan Jenkins

QUESTIONS TO FACILITATE UNDERSTANDING THE IMPACT

(The following questions refer to abusive fathers. They may be reworded for other contexts).

CONFUSION

How would it feel to be innocent and little and to be tricked/forced into something secret you don't understand, by your father whom you love/trust?

What would it feel like to have your father doing secret things to you, that you know are wrong but just don't understand?

What would it be like to have your father saying its O.K. and giving you stuff for doing bad things?

What would it feel like to be told it's O.K. but then told to keep it secret or else?

FEAR

What would it feel like if you were forced to do something bad that hurts you, by your father?

What would it feel like to be threatened or told that terrible things will happen if you don't do it?

What would it feel like to be threatened or told that terrible things will happen if you tell?

What would it feel like to be always thinking:
- Is it going to happen tonight?
- Is he going to hurt me again?
- If I don't do it/tell, he will hurt me?
- If I don't do it will he stop loving me?

TRAPPED

What would it feel like to be the only person that knows about it?

What would it feel like to know that you can't hide or resist or stop it because your father is much bigger, stronger and cleverer than you?

How would it feel to have gone along with your father's secret 'games' at first but realise now that you are right out of your depth?

What would it feel like to think that if you tell:
- No-one will believe you

- You will get into big trouble
- You will have to go to a home to live
- You will split up your mum and dad/family
- Your dad will go to gaol
- Your dad will get depressed/upset/leave you or mum.

SHAME/SELF-BLAME/GUILT

What would it be like to be only ... years old but treated as though you are old enough to choose to have sex before you even know what sex is?
- Who would you think is responsible?

What would it be like to be only ... years old and have it left up to you to set limits?
- Who would you think is responsible for what happens?

What would it be like to be too young to realize that you have been tricked and too young to know any better?
- Who would you think is responsible?

What would it be like to have to carry your father's secret at ... years of age?
- Who would you think is responsible?

What would it feel like if you initially went along with your father and later found yourself having to do things you didn't like?

How would it make you feel about yourself?
- Who would you blame?

What would it feel like if at first you even liked the secret 'games' your father started?

Who would you think is responsible?

What would it feel like to know you have accepted favors or things in return for sex?

How would this make you feel about yourself?

If you believed that you were also responsible for something that is very bad and very naughty, how would you feel about yourself?

How would you start to see yourself?

How could this make it hard for you to feel angry at your father?

How would you be likely to feel instead?

BURDEN OF RESPONSIBILITY

What would it feel like to carry such a big secret around for so long?

What would it feel like to be bribed and threatened not to tell?

Alan Jenkins

215

-   What would it be like to carry this responsibility, for your dad and
    your family, single-handed at the age of....?
What would it feel like to be only ... years old and have to carry around
your father's problems on your shoulders?
What would it do to you?
What would it feel like to be constantly worried about being abused,
keeping the secret, what people will think of you - so that you can't relax
and get on with living your own life?
What would it feel like to be only ... years old and have to be the one
that does something to stop it?
What would you be up against?
What would it feel like to try to bring yourself to tell?
What would it feel like to actually tell on your father?

BETRAYAL/USED/ANGER

What would it be like to be a child, if the only special times your dad
put aside to show caring for you were muddled up with sexual abuse?
What would it do to you to be called a liar and be blamed for your
father's problem when you finally plucked up courage to tell?
What would it feel like to realize that your father just used you and
didn't care about your feelings?
How would it feel to realize that your father tricked you into sexual
abuse, that he planned it and kept you trapped in it for ... years?

SELF-ESTEEM

If you believed that the abuse was your fault too, how would this make
you feel about yourself?
How would you start to see yourself?
What would it do to your confidence?
If your father used you and treated you as though your feelings and
rights were not important:
What message would this give you about yourself?
How would you start to see yourself?
How would you start to think others see you?
How would you start to treat yourself with others?
What would it be like trying to grow up, if you felt you had to be your
father's person and look after his feelings and problems, rather than be
your own person and take care of your own concerns?

FUTURE LIFESTYLE

What would it feel like when you were old enough to realize what your father really did to you and how much you have been used by your own father?

What would it feel like to realize that your father had dumped his problems on you and expected you to carry them for him?

How would you look back on your father?

What would it feel like to discover that your father believed that you really enjoyed or benefited from his abuse?

What would it feel like to realize that you have been robbed of your right to decide on your first sexual experience?

What would it feel like to be carrying the secret everywhere you go - at school, with friends - everywhere?

What would it be like to be constantly worried whether people will know or can tell?

What would it be like trying to make friends?

As a girl:

How would you feel about relating to boys after your experience with your father?

What message would your father have given you about trusting men?

If your father ignored your feelings and your rights and was only interested in your body:

What message would this give you about what men want from relationships with girls?

What would it say about what men think is important about girls?

What message does it give about how to get close to a men?

What training would your father have given you about what woman/wives/daughters should be like/should do?

What example would he have shown you about what husbands/fathers are really like?

How could this training effect your future?

As a boy:

What training would your father have given you about what men/fathers/husbands should be like/should do?

What example would he set for you about how to relate to kids/others?

How could this training effect your future?

Alan Jenkins

FACILITATING UNDERSTANDING OF THE PATTERN OF OFFENDING

Relate questions to specific incidents.

FIRST INCIDENT
ANTECEDENTS

When did you first abuse (the victim)?
What was happening at the time?
Where were you? Where was (the victim)?
What were you doing?
What had you been doing previously?
What was (the victim) doing?
What sort of mood were you in?
How were you feeling?
- happy/angry/sad/scared/hurt/rejected/lonely/trapped/ unsuccessful/a failure/sexually aroused
What had happened to make you feel that way?
What were you thinking at the time?
- about yourself?
- about (the victim)?
- about sex?
What triggered off this thinking?
What were you really wanting?

PLANNING --> EXECUTION

How did you start to plan the abuse?
What did you start to think?
What did you start to imagine/fantasize/daydream about?
What pictures/stories did you have in your mind?
- about (the victim)?
- about yourself?
How did these make you feel?
What did you start to do?
What did (the victim) do?
What did you then think/do/feel? etc.

PRE-PLANNING

What were the initial warning signs before this, indicating that you might do it?

When did you first think about sexually abusing before this?

When did you first imagine these pictures/stories?

Who were you imagining in these pictures/stories?
- (the victim)/others?

When did you first read about it/watch it on TV?
- What did you think/feel?

When did you first imagine/think about sexually harassing/assaulting someone yourself?
- When did you first try it out?
- How did you feel?

VICTIM CHOICE

Why did you choose (the victim)?

What was it about (the victim) that made him/her a good target?

What attracted you to (the victim)?
- appearance/age/gender/size/naivety/innocence/easy?

FANTASY SCRIPT

What was the abuse like in your imagination?

What did you hope it would be like?
- How did you hope you would feel?
- How did you hope (the victim) would feel?
- What did you imagine would feel good for you?
- How did you hope (the victim) would feel about you?
- How did you hope others would feel about you?

AFTERMATH

What was it actually like?

How did it make you feel about yourself?

What did you say to yourself/think afterwards?

What did you say/do to (the victim) afterwards?

JUSTIFICATIONS

How did you try to justify/explain away your abuse?
- in the face of (the victim's) distress?

(see levels of denial of responsibility - Figure 1)

What was the 'good part'/moral side/mature side of you saying about the abuse?

What was the 'bad part'/immoral side of you saying about the abuse?

What stories/pictures did you make about the abuse to help you to knock out your good/moral side?

SUBSEQUENT INCIDENTS

When did you last (offend)?

(go through previous questions as for first incident)

How did you plan/set up opportunities to (offend)?

Has your abuse got heavier/more frequent/more dangerous/involved more victims over time?
- What is the trend?

Have you been feeling more and more in control of it or more and more out of control over time?

How have you been feeling afterwards each time?
- about (the victim)/about yourself?
- What is the trend over time?

SEX ABUSE TRAINING

When did you last feel like (offending)?
- What did you do?
- Are you getting more in charge or are you becoming more and more hooked?

When did you last catch yourself planning to abuse?
- How far had you progressed?
- Did you/do you think you could have stopped yourself?
- How?

When did you last catch yourself 'perving' at young kids/(the victim)?

When did you last catch yourself masturbating to thoughts/pictures in your mind of young kids/(the victim)?
- What happens in these fantasies?
- Is this happening more often or less often?

- Do you think you could stop yourself using these fantasies or are you too hooked/addicted?

When did you last catch yourself masturbating to fantasies that are exploitative, violent or weird?

When did you last catch yourself reading or looking at material about kids and feeling sexually aroused/interested?

When did you last catch yourself sexually harassing someone or trying to make them feel uncomfortable?

- Are you doing this more often or less often?

Are you training harder and harder for a career as a sex offender or are you practising for a new lifestyle?

How are you trying to quit?

- ,avoid sex/masturbation/sexual thoughts
- distraction from sexual thoughts/keeping busy
- avoid temptation
- feeling guilty/harassing self re sexual thoughts.

RESTRAINTS ACTIVE AT DIFFERENT LEVELS OF CONTEXT

Socio-Cultural		Traditional Gender Myths - status & entitlement - social-emotional responsibility
Developmental	Family of Origin - parental incompetence abuse/neglect - responsibility over/under loads Peer Group - abuse/bullying	Training in Social Emotional Avoidance - responsibility over/under loads - peer relations - bullying - withdrawal
Interactional	Broader Context of Parental Incompetence - abuse/neglect/ irresponsibility - unrealistic expectations - inappropriate alliances - failure to respect boundaries - parenting responsibility imbalances	Marital Relationship Imbalance - power/status - responsibility Reliance on Victim/Partner - to face social emot.pressures & responsibilities
Individual	Pattern of Abusive Behaviour patterns of - deception - exploitation - justification - attribution of responsibility - fantasy	Social-Emotional "Immaturity" - self-centred thinking - avoid/withdraw from responsib. - insensitivity - poor relationship skills

RESTRAINTS ACTIVE AT DIFFERENT LEVELS OF CONTEXT

Cultural Myths re Male Self-Esteem	Cultural Myths re Male Sexuality	Cultural Myths re Sexual & Emotional Irresponsibility
- status - sexual conquest	- performance & conquest - sex = intimacy	

Training in Social Inadequacy	Training in Sexual Exploitation	Training in Avoidance of Responsibility

- peer rejection & withdrawal
- history of bullying/ harrassment
	- sexual history
	  - abuse
	  - harrassment
	  - sexual problems and concerns
		- reliance on others/ blame
		- emotional avoidance

Reliance on Victim	Reliance on Victim/ Partner	Reliance on Victim
The man is propped up by the victim who - conforms to his needs/fantasies - makes no demand - is vulnerable/ naive/dependent - keeps the secret Reliance on Partner - submission/deference	The man is not threatened by the victim - performance/fears - justifications - sexual myths & beliefs protected by secrecy The man relies on partner's support & tolerance of his sexual interests	The man attributes responsibility to the victim - tricked into participation - keeps secret - justifications - setting limits & stopping abuse Victim cannot decline - attends to abuse for the man

Poor Self Esteem	Sexual Preoccupation	Misguided Efforts to Deal with Abuse

- preoccupation with adequacy
- compensation
  -status displays
  -withdrawal into fantasy
	- confusion of sex with needs for:
	  - affirmation
	  - closeness/affect
	  - status/control
	- low interpersonal requirements in sex
	- misguided beliefs fears/doubts
		- inadvertent maintenance practices
		- avoidance & distraction
		  - abuse
		  - own needs
		  - justifications
		  - attribution of responsibility
		  - confusion urge/action

Alan Jenkins

LETTER OF APOLOGY

REASON FOR WRITING
- statement of the man's concern/caring for (the victim's) feelings about his abuse

  "I am writing to you because I am feeling ... about how I have treated you"

  "I am writing to you because I am feeling ... about you and ... about what I have put you through"

STATEMENT OF APOLOGY
- details of sexual abuse

  "I am very sorry for touching your private parts and making you touch mine"

  as opposed to " ... for what I did"
- details of other abuse, harassment etc.

  "I am very sorry for making you ... and calling you ... when ... "
- not facing up

  "I am very sorry for threatening to ... if you told/making you keep such a terrible secret:

  "I am very sorry for calling you a liar/threatening you when you told ...?"

STATEMENT OF RESPONSIBILITY
- Who is responsible?

  "It is all my fault - it is not your fault"

  "I believe that I am fully responsible"
- Why?

  "I am your father - you trusted me"

  "I should not have made you do it but should have instead ... - you were not old enough/strong enough to stop me - I made you too frightened to be able to stop it"

  "I should never have tricked you into it by pretending ... /by giving you ..."
- I knew it was a trick but you didn't
- you couldn't help being tricked
- you didn't know it was wrong

- I knew how to stop it but you didn't know
- you were trapped by me
- What should have happened?
  "I wasn't a proper father to you"
  "Big people (especially fathers) should look after/protect/help younger kids rather than hurt them or trick them into bad things"
- Statement re the victim's disclosure
  "I think you did a very good and a very brave thing in telling ..."
  "Telling someone is the best thing to do if someone is hurting you - now you are getting some help and I am getting some help"
  "Kids don't have to put up with being hurt and pushed around by bigger people"

STATEMENT OF UNDERSTANDING OF IMPACT
- abuse itself
- secrecy
- being dumped with responsibility
  "I am starting to realize some of what I must have put you through"
  "it must have been ... to be made to ..."
  "You must have felt confused/mixed up when I ..."
- told you it was O.K.
- told you to keep it secret
- told you I would go to gaol if you tell
  "I must have frightened/terrified you by ..."
- making threats
- violence/verbal abuse/hurting you
- keeping on coming in your room when you didn't want me to
  "You must have felt trapped when ..."
  "I betrayed you by ... "
- taking advantage of your trust
- putting my feelings before yours - using you
- treating you like a thing to be used
- as though your feelings and wishes don't matter
- abusing our father/child relationship
- not being sensitive to your feelings when ...
- not facing up when you told
- violating your privacy/your body
  "I tried to cop out and make you feel responsible too, by ... "

Alan Jenkins

- dumping my problems on to your shoulders and making you carry them for me
- telling you it was OK - tricking you into it
- giving you favors if you did it
- treating you as if you were an equal partner who is able to give your consent
- leaving it up to you to set limits/say "No"
- making you keep it secret and carry that secret for ... years
- making you think terrible things would happen to you/me if you told

STATEMENT OF WHAT YOU ARE DOING ABOUT IT
- Receiving help
  "I am seeing a counsellor so that I can make sure that nothing like this will ever happen again"
  "I am learning to face up to and understand what I did"
  "I am trying to understand what I have put you through"
- Statement about distancing
- why distance/who is responsible
  "I am living somewhere else so that I can completely face up to my problem and give you time and space to deal with what I have done to you"
  "I have decided to move out/I agree with the welfare because it is my problem and I need to be 100 percent sure I have fixed it before I live with you again"

RECURRENCES
- Statement re consequences
- Readiness and ability to face consequences
  "I am no longer trying to cop out from taking responsibility. I know that I have committed a crime as well as having betrayed you. I am ready/can handle whatever consequences that I will have to face. This is not your responsibility"

STATEMENT OF FUTURE INTENT
  "I will never sexually abuse you or anyone else again"
  "I won't let anyone else hurt you - I will protect you"
  "I am going to be a proper father to you from now on - I won't hurt you or touch your private parts"

"I would like the opportunity to meet with you and ... to apologize in person"

"I am not asking for you to forgive me - I just want to let you know how I am feeling about what I did to you"

"I believe that you have every right to feel angry and betrayed"

"I don't need you to keep secrets for me/pretend/try to look after my feelings any more"

REFERENCES

Abel, G.G., Becker, J.V., Cunningham-Rathner, J., Mittelman, M. & Rouleau, J.L. (1988).
"Multiple paraphilic diagnoses among sex offenders." **Bull. Am. Acad. Psychiatry Law**, 16(2):153-168.

Abel, G.G., Mittelman, M., Becker, J.V., Cunningham-Rathner, J. & Lucas, I. (1983).
"The characteristics of men who molest children." Paper presented at the **World Congress of Behaviour Therapy**, Washington.

Alexander, P.C. (1985).
"A systems theory conceptual theory of incest." **Family Process**, 24:19-88.

Araji, S. & Finkelhor, D. (1986).
"Abusers: a review of the research" in Finkelhor, D. (ed.) **A Sourcebook on Child Sexual Abuse**. California, Sage Publications.

Bateson, G. (1972).
Steps to an Ecology of Mind. New York, Ballantine Books.

Bateson, G. (1980).
Mind and Nature: A necessary unity. New York, Bantam Books.

Baxter, J. (1988).
"The sexual division of labor in Australian families." **Australian Journal of Sex, Marriage and Family**, 9: 87-93.

Bograd, M (1984).
"Family systems approaches to wife battering: a feminist critique." **American Journal of Orthopsychiatry**, 54(4):558-568.

Brennen, F.A. 1985.
"Political and psychosocial issues in psychotherapy for spouse abusers: implications for treatments." **Psychotherapy,** 22(3):643-654.

Broussard, M.S. & Wagner, W.G. (1988).
"Child sexual abuse: who is to blame?" **Child Abuse and Neglect,** 12:563-569.

Bulky, J. & Davidson, H.A. (1981).
"Child sexual abuse: legal issues and approaches." **American Bar Association,** Washington.

Burt, M.R. (1980).
"Cultural myths and supports for rape." **Journal of Personality and Social Psychology,** 38:2317-230.

Cashmore, J. & Horsky, M. (1987).
"Child sexual assault: the court response." **N.S.W. Bureau of Crime Statistics and Research,** Sydney.

Ceck, J.V.P. & Malamuth, N.W. (1983).
"Sex role stereotyping and reactions to depictions of stranger versus acquaintance rape." **Journal of Personality and Social Psychology,** 45:344-356.

Cook, D.R. & Frantz-Cook, A. (1984).
"A systemic approach to wife battering." **Journal of Marital and Family Therapy,** 10(1):830-93.

Deschner, J.P. (1984).
The Hitting Habit: Anger control for battering couples. Plenum Press, New York.

de Young, M. (1982).
Sexual Victimization of Children. MacFarlane, Jefferson, NC.

Dobash, E.R. & Dobash, R (1979).
Violence Against Wives : A case against the patriarchy. Free
Press, New York.

Earls, C.M. (1988).
"Aberrant sexual arousal in sexual offenders" in Prentky, R.A. &
Quinsey, V.L. (eds.) **Human Sexual Aggression: Current
perspectives.** Annals New York Academy of Sciences, 528:41-48.

Finkelhor, D. (1983).
"Common features of family abuse" in Finkelhor, D., Gelles, R.J.,
Hotaling, G.T., & Straus, M.A. (eds.) **The Dark Side of Families:
Current family violence research.** Sage Publications, Beverly Hills.

Finkelhor, D. & Araji, S. (1986).
"Explanations of pedophilia: a four factor model." **Journal of Sex
Research,** 22(2):145-161.

Finkelhor, D. & Lewis, J.A. (1988).
"An epidemiologic approach to the study of child molestation" in
Prentky, R.A. & Quinsey, V.L. (eds.) **Human Sexual Aggression:
Current perspectives.** Academy of Sciences, New York.

Friedman, S. (1988).
"A family systems approach to treatment" in Walker, L.E. (ed.)
**Handbook on Sexual Abuse of Children: Assessment and
treatment issues.** Springer Publishing Co, New York.

Furman, B. & Ahola, T. (1988).
"Return of the question "why": advantages of exploring pre-existing
explanations." **Family Process,** 27:395-409.

Gelles, R.J. (1980).
"Violence in the family: a review of research in the seventies."
Journal of Marriage and the Family, 42:873-885.

Gelles, R.J. & Cornell, C.P. (1985).
Intimate Violence In Families. Sage Publications, California.

Gentemann, K.M. (1984).
"Wife beating: attitudes of a non-clinical population."
Victimology, 9:109-119.

Giaretto, H. (1981).
"A comprehensive child sexual abuse treatment programme" in
Mrazek, P.B. & Kempe, C.H. (eds.) **Sexually Abused Children
and their Families.** Pergamon, New York.

Glasser, W.F. (1988).
"'Treatment' or 'sentence' for child molestors: a comparison of
Australian offenders with a general prison population." **Int. J. Law
Psychiatry,** 11:145-156.

Gobhard, P.H., Gagnon, J.H., Pomeroy, W.B., & Christenson, C.V.
(1965).
Sex Offenders: An analysis of types. Harpers & Row, New York.

Gondolf, E.W. (1985).
**Men Who Batter: An integrated approach for stopping wife
abuse.** Florida, Learning Publication.

Gondolf, E.W. (1987).
"Evaluating programmes for men who batter: problems and
prospects." **Journal of Family Violence,** 2(1):95-108.

Gondolf, E.W. (1987).
"Changing men who batter: a developmental model for integrated
interventions." **Journal of Family Violence,** 2(4):335-349.

Gondolf, E.W. & Hanneken, J. (1987).
"The gender warrior: reformed batterers on abuse, treatment and
change." **Journal of Family Violence,** 2(1):177-191.

Greenblatt, C.S. (1985).
"Don't hit your wife ... unless ...: preliminary findings on
normative support for the use of physical force by husbands."
Victimology, 10:221-241.

Gross, A.E. (1978).
"The male role and heterosexual behaviour." **Journal of Social
Issues**, 34:87-107.

Groth, A.N. (1979).
Men Who Rape: The psychology of the offender. Plenum Press,
New York.

Groth, A.N. (1982).
"The incest offender" in Sgroi, S.M. (ed.) **Handbook of Clinical
Intervention in Child Sexual Abuse**. Lexington Books,
Massachusetts.

Groth, A.N. & Burgess, A.W. (1979).
"Sexual trauma in the life histories of rapists and child molesters."
Victimology, 4:10-16.

Groth, A. & Cohen, M. (1979).
"Aggressive sexual offenders: diagnosis and treatment" in Burgess,
(ed.) **Community Mental Health**. Prentice Hall, Englewood Cliffs.

Groth, A.N., Hobson, W. & Gary, T. (1982).
"The child molester: clinical observations" in Conte, J. & Shore, D.
(eds.) **Social Work and Child Sexual Abuse**. Haworth, New York.

Groth, A.N., Longo, R.E., & McFadin, J.B. (1982).
"Undetected recidivism among rapists and child molestors." **Crime
and Delinquency**, 28(3):450-458.

Haley, J. (1963).
Strategies of Psychotherapy. Grune & Stratton, New York.

Alan Jenkins

Hamberger, L.K. & Hastings, J.E. (1986).
"Personality correlates of men who abuse their partners: a cross-validation study." **Journal of Family Violence**, 1(4):323-341.

Hite, S. (1981).
The Hite Report on Male Sexuality. Knoop, New York.

Hoffman, L. (1981).
Foundations of Family Therapy. Basic Books, New York.

Hotaling, G.T. & Sugarman, D.B. (1986).
"An analysis of risk markers in husband to wife violence." **Viol. Victims**, 1:101-124.

Jenkins, M.J. & Dambrot, F.H. (1987).
"The attribution of date rape: observer's attitudes and sexual experiences and the dating situation." **Journal of Applied Social Psychology**, 17(10):875-895.

Jennings, J.L. 1987.
"History and issues in the treatment of battering men: a case for unstructured group therapy. **Journal of Family Violence**, 2(3):193-213.

Justice, B. & Justice, R. (1979).
The Broken Taboo: Sex in the family. Human Sciences Press, New York.

Kanin, E.J. (1985).
"Date rapists: differential sexual socialization and relative deprivation." **Archives of Sexual Behaviour**, 14:219-231.

Kantor, G.K. & Straus, M.A. (1987).
"The 'drunken bum' theory of wife beating." **Social Problems**, 34(3):212-230.

Klein, D. (1981).
"Violence against women: some considerations regarding its causes and its elimination." **Crime and Delinquency**, January, 1981.

Knopp, F.H. (1982).
Remedial Intervention in Adolescent Sex Offences: Nine program descriptions. Safer Society Press, New York.

Knopp, F.H. (1984).
Retraining Adult Sex Offenders: Methods and models. Safer Society Press, New York.

Koss, M.P., Leonard, K.E., Beezley, D.A. & Oros, C.J. (1985).
"Nonstranger sexual aggression: a discriminant analysis of the psychological characteristics of undetected offenders." **Sex Roles**, 12(9/10):981-992.

Krausz, S.L. (1986).
"Sex roles within marriage." **Social Work**, 17:457-464.

Langevin, R. (1975).
Erotic Preference, Gender Identity and Aggression in Men: New research studies. Lawrence Erlbaum Assocs, New Jersey.

Larson, N.R. & Maddock, J.W. (1986).
"Structural and functional variables in incest family systems" in Trepper, T.S. & Barret, M.J. (eds.) **Treating Incest: A multimodal systems perspective.** Haworth Press, New York.

Leitenberg, H., Greenwald, E. & Tarran, M.J. (1989).
"The relation between sexual activity among children during pre-adolescence and/or early adolescence and sexual behaviour and sexual adjustment in young adulthood." **Archives of Sexual Behaviour**, 18(4):299-313.

Levin, S.M. & Stava, L. (1987).
"Personality characteristics of sex offenders: a review." **Archives of Sexual Behaviour**, 16(1):57-79.

Levine, E.M. (1986).
"Sociocultural causes of family violence: a theoretical comment." **Journal of Family Violence**, 1(1):3-12.

Lisak, D. & Roth, S. (1988).
"Motivational factors in non-incarcerated sexually aggressive men." **Journal of Personality and Social Psychology**, 55(5):795-802.

Lustig, L., Dresser, J.W., Spellman, S.W. & Murray, T.B. (1966).
"Incest: a family group survival pattern." **Archives of General Psychiatry**, 14:31-40.

Machotka, P., Pittman, F.S. & Flomenhaft, K. (1967).
"Incest as a family affair." **Family Process**, 6:98-116.

Madden, D.J. (1982).
"Adolescent violence in the family" in Hansen, J.C. (ed.) **Clinical Approaches to Family Violence**. Aspen Systems to, London.

Malamuth, N.M. (1986).
"Predictors of naturalistic sexual aggression." **Journal of Personality and Social Psychology**, 50(5):953-962.

Margolin, L., Morgan, P.B. & Miller, M. (1989).
"Social approval for violations of sexual consent in marriage and dating." **Violence and Victims**, 4(1):45-55.

Marolla, J.A. & Scully, D.H. (1979).
"Rape and psychiatric vocabularies of motive" in Gomberg, E. & Franks, V. (eds.) **Gender and Disordered Behaviour**. Brunner/Mazel, New York.

McFarlane, K. & Buckley, J. (1982).
"Treating child sexual abuse: an overview of current program models" in **Social Work and Child Sexual Abuse**. Haworth Press.

McGuire, R.J., Carlisle, J.M. & Young B.G. (1965).
"Sexual deviations and conditioned behaviour: a hypothesis." **Behaviour Research and Therapy**, 2:1850-190.

McIntyre, D. (1984).
"Domestic violence: a case of the disappearing victim." **Australian Journal of Family Therapy**, 5(4):249-258.

Metcalf, A. & Humphries, M. (eds.) (1985).
The Sexuality of Men. Pluto Press, London.
National Committee on Violence. (1990).
Violence: Directions for Australia. Australian Institute of Criminology, Canberra.

Neidig, P.H., Friedman, D.H. & Collins, B. (1985).
"Domestic conflict containment: a spouse abuse treatment programme." **Social Casework: The Journal of Contemporary Social Work**, 66(4):195-204.

Overholser, J.C. & Beck, S. (1986).
"Multimethod assessment of rapists, child molesters and three control groups on behavioural and psychological measures." **Journal of Consulting and Clinical Psychology**, 54(5):682-687.

Parker, H. & Parker, S. (1986).
"Father-daughter abuse: an emerging perspective." **American Journal of Orthopsychiatry**, 56(4):531-549.

Perry, M.A., Wells, E.A. & Doran, L.D. (1983).
"Parent characteristics in abusing and non-abusing families." **Journal of Clinical and Child Psychology**, 12:329-336.

Person, E.J. (1980).
"Sexuality as the mainstay of identity." **Signs**, 5:605-630.

Prepper, A. (1984).
"The invisible reality: patterns and power in family violence" in Baker, M. (ed.) **The Family: changing trends in Canada**. McGraw-Hill, Toronto.

Public Policy Research Centre (1988).
Community Attitudes Towards Domestic Violence in Australia. Department of the Prime Minister & Cabinet, Office of the Status of Women. Canberra.

Queensland Domestic Violence Taskforce Report (1988).
Beyond These Walls. Report of the Queensland Domestic Violence Taskforce, Brisbane, October 1988.

Radan, R.T. (1976).
"Alcoholism and the child molester." **Annals of New York Academy of Science**, 273:492-496.

Raphling, D.L., Carpenter, B.L. & Davis, A. (1967).
"Incest: A genealogical study." **Archives of General Psychiatry**, 16:505-511.

Rist, K. (1979).
"Incest: theoretical and clinical views." **American Journal of Orthopsychiatry**, 49:680-691.

Roscoe, B., Callahan, J.E. & Peterson, K.L. (1985).
"Who is responsible? Adolescent's acceptance of theoretical child abuse models." **Adolescence**, 20(77):189-197.

Rosenbaum, A. (1986).
"Family violence" in Curran, W.J., McGarry, A.L. & Shah, S.A. (eds.) **Forensic Psychiatry and Psychology**. Davis, Philadelphia.

Rosenbaum, A. (1986).
"Of men, macho and marital violence." **Journal of Family Violence,** 1(2):121-129.

Rosenbaum, A. & O'Leary, K.D. (1981).
"Marital violence: characteristics of abusive couples." **Journal of Consulting and Clinical Psychology,** 49(1):63-71.

Roy, M. (1982).
"The nature of abusive behaviour" in Roy, M. (ed.) **The Abusive Partner.** Van Nostrand Reinhold, New York.

Rush, F. (1980).
The Best Kept Secret: Sexual abuse of children. Prentice-Hall, New Jersey.

Russell, D.E. (1974).
The Politics of Rape. Stein and Day, New York
Russell, D.E. (1984).
Sexual Exploitation : Rape, child sexual abuse and workplace harassment. Sage Publications, Beverley Hills.

Russell, M. (1988).
"Wife assault theory, research and treatment: a literature review." **Journal of Family Violence,** 3(3):193-208

Saunders, E.B. & Awad, G.A. (1988).
"Assessment, management and treatment for male adolescent sexual offenders." **American Journal of Orthopsychiatry,** 58(4):571-579

Sattem, L., Savells, J. & Murray, E. (1984).
"Sex role stereotypes and commitment of rape." **Sex Roles,** 11(9/10):849-860.

Schechter, S. (1982).
Women and Male Violence: The visions and struggles of the Battered Women's Movement. South: Boston.

Segal, Z.V. & Marshall, W.L. (1985).
"Heterosexual social skills in a population of rapists and child molesters." **Journal of Consulting and Clinical Psychology,** 53(1):55-63.

Shupe, A., Stacey, W.A. & Hazlewood, L.R. (1987).
Violent Men, Violent Couples: The dynamics of domestic violence. Lexington Books: Toronto.

Snell, J.E., Rosenwald, R.J. & Rosey, A. (1964).
"The wifebeater's wife: a study of family interactions." **Archives of General Psychiatry,** 11:107-113

Sommers-Flanagan, R.S. & Walters, H.A. (1987).
"The incest offender, power and victimization: scales on the same dragon." **Journal of Family Violence,** 2(2):163-175.

Sonkin, D.J., Martin, D. & Walker L.E.A. (1985).
The Male Batterer - A treatment approach. Springer Publishing Co, New York.

South Australian Health Commission (1986).
South Australian Government Task Force on Child Sexual Abuse. Adelaide.

Stets, J.E. & Pirog-Good, M.A. (1989).
"Pattern of physical and sexual abuse for men and women in dating relationships: a descriptive analysis." **Journal of Family Violence,** 4(1):63-76.

Storr, A. (1970).
Human Aggression. Bantam Books, New York

Straus, M.A., Gelles, R.J. & Steinmetz, S.K. (1980).
Behind Closed Doors. Anchor Books, New York.

Summit, R. & Kryso, J. (1978).
"Sexual abuse of children: a clinical spectrum." **American J. of Orthopsychiatry**, 48:2.

Taubman, S. (1986).
"Beyond the bravado: sex roles and the exploitive male." **Social Work**, 31(2):12-18.

Tavris, C. (1982).
Anger: The misunderstood emotion. Simon & Schuster, New York.

Telch, C.F. & Lindquist, C.V. (1984).
"Violent versus nonviolent couples: a comparison of patterns." **Psychotherapy: theory, practice & research**, 21:242-248.

Walker, L.E. (1984).
The Battered Woman Syndrome. Springer Publishing Co, New York.

Weitzman, J. & Dreen, K. (1982).
"Wife beating: a view of the marital dyad." **Social Casework**. 63:259-265.

Will, D. (1983).
"Approaching the incestuous and sexually abusive family." **Journal of Adolescence**, 6:229-246

White, M. (1984).
"Marital therapy: practical approaches to longstanding problems." **Australian Journal of Family Therapy**, 5(1):27-43.

White, M. (1986a).
"Negative explanation, restraint & double description: a template for family therapy." **Family Process**, 22:255-273.

White, M. (1986b).
"Anorexia nervosa: a cybernetic perspective" in Elka-Harkaway, J (ed.) **Eating Disorders**. Maryland, Aspen Publishers.

White, M. (1988).
"The process of questioning: a therapy of literary merit?" **Dulwich Centre Newsletter**, Winter 1988.

White, M. (1989).
"The externalizing of the problem and the re-authoring of lives and relationships." **Dulwich Centre Newsletter**, Summer 1988/89.

Yourell, A.M. & McCabe, M.P. (1988).
"The motivation underlying male rape of women." **Australian Journal of Sex, Marriage & Family**, 9(4):215-224.

Zilbergeld, B. (1978).
Male Sexuality. Bantam, New York.

⇒ for pt it is his responsibility